# From Dusk 'til

# Dawn

*It's Not What You See, it's What God Says*

# From Dusk 'til Dawn

Book Printed by Amazon Kindle Direct Publishing

ISBN: 9798846725713

Cover Design by Wink and Ann West

Cover Photo by Lovell and Jackie White

Author Photo by Lawrence Smith, Czar Photography

All Scripture references, unless otherwise indicated, are taken from the Holy Bible, New Living Translation (NLT), or other versions as indicated.

# CONTENT

DEDICATION / v

ACKNOWLEDGEMENTS / viii

FORWARD / xv

PREFACE / xix

Chapter 1 / 1 – In the Beginning

Outtake

Chapter 2 /16 –Who's to Blame

Outtake

Chapter 3 / 32 – The Search

Outtake

Chapter 4 / 53 – Still Searching

Outtake

Chapter 5 / 69 – Heart Check

Outtake

Chapter 6 / 91 – Next Stop

Outtake

# CONTENT (CONT.)

Chapter 7 / 109 - The Call

    Outtake

Chapter 8 / 124 – Is This my Hand

    Outtake

Chapter 9 / 138 – Pushing the Envelope

    Outtake

Shawn and Sherrod's Outtake / 159

Evolution of a Miracle / 166

Where to Find Wink / 168

The **Outtakes** after each chapter in the book are meant to give readers a look at the running tape behind the scenes of our lives. They are also thoughts running through my mind as God plotted and directed each scene. You don't want to leave each chapter and go on to the next without experiencing the outtakes. When we see them in movies they add flavor to the story. Our hope is that you experience the same after reading ours.

# DEDICATIONS

## "My Better Half"

To Ann, my best friend, teenage sweetheart, forever queen, and love of my life. This book could have easily been named *"The book Ann has been waiting on – it's about time"*. You have read this manuscript more than a dozen times as I edited and re-edited its content. Thank you for pushing me and showing grace and patience. You did it not just for this work, but for our lives. If it were not for you, there would be no us. Thank you for pointing out what you see in me so many times before I see it in myself. You have always encouraged me when I lacked the drive to finish strong. Words escape me when I think of how many ways you continue to help me grow. I'm amazed at how quietly and excellently you lead. You are like that quiet storm that settles right at the point of impact. Thank you so much for loving me the way you do. I can never repay you for how you have helped change how I think. I remember those vows we made as teens on the porch and then at the altar. I can thank you by living my life the way I promised you I would. The journey we traveled in the pages of this book helped refocus me to keep my promise. You deserve the life you prayed and dreamed about. God honored your prayer! You are my ride or die forever and ever amen! Take a bow! God continues to write our story.

**Mott and Joan Spruell** (deceased), mom and pop, I dedicate this book to you for the countless times you walked me through life's challenges. I heard you cheering from the stands on many occasions. Thank you so much for the example you were for me for so long. Your labor was not in vain. You told me if I put God first, my life would be most fulfilled. You were right AGAIN! This one is for you.

# ACKNOWLEDGEMENTS

I am a firm believer that the successes we encounter in life are rarely, if at all, solo acts. There are people on our paths that are divinely appointed for whatever season you are in to help you win. Many of them you would have never placed on your "go to" list. Some are unassuming and others are forthright. They are not named specifically in the book, but their actions are captured in the story we tell. It is here where we would like to honor them for all they did to help the West Family throughout this journey. They come from various walks of life, nationalities and cultures. Many of them will never meet or cross paths, but they so uniquely fit together for this purpose.

**God**, we thank you first for obvious reasons. You are the beginning and ending of everything. Without you, there is no story; this is why you get all the glory. The reason we exist is because of you.

Thank you for allowing our family to experience your grace, love and character. Thank you for trusting us. Mom often tried to articulate your incredible nature. You handed us tickets to front row seats and backstage passes. What a performance! You did not disappoint. You must really love us! Thank you for surrounding our family with people who love you and served us well.

**Dr. Cliff Ashe III**, thank you for being that sounding board and counsel I needed during some difficult times. You did what pastors do; you pointed me to Jesus and encouraged me to stay strong and take my rightful position as a man to cover my family. You told me to stay in the fight. You were my "cut man". Thank you for dressing my wounds. You earned the name as a man's man and coach.

**Walter** (deceased) **and Renee Butler,** your home and hearts were a safe haven for Sherrod on countless occasions. Your love for him and us during some of our darkest days will never be forgotten. We called on you often, and you responded each and every time without question. Walter, you treated Sherrod as if he were your own son. He loved you dearly and still speaks of you today. Renee, you welcomed him like a mother and always had a place for him at the table. We owe you for him eating all your great food, especially the potato salad.

**Jonathan and Jasmine Butler**, thank you for loving Sherrod like a brother and letting him hang out day or night whenever possible. Your friendship was invaluable for his mental and social health. You two were awesome friends for him.

**Leonard (LC) and Carolyn Caston**, thank you for walking with us, praying with us and accompanying us to the hospital emergency room that one frightening night. Your connection to God kept us connected to God.

**Mr. Milford Pittman** (deceased), you were the counselor Sherrod needed in middle school. He escaped some of the jeers and negative comments from peers because of your open-door policy that gave him the outlet he needed when he needed it.

**Ms. Dottie Fitton**, you helped make Sherrod's transition from one middle school to yours less challenging for the family. You cared for him in a very loving and unique way. Thank you for your heart.

**Dr. Yanick Vibert**, you were the angel God sent at the right place at the right time when we admitted Sherrod into the hospital for psychiatric evaluation. We were in a very fragile place at that time, and you stilled the waters of our storm with your presence. You were a trusted adviser and friend. You watched while we rested.

**James and Stephanie Lyles**, you sensed we needed rest early on in this journey. We were literally exhausted the night he packed an overnight bag to come stay with you. How can we forget that night? Although the night ended early; Sherrod was so excited about that sleepover and so were we. I think you are the only one who has ever called the police on me.

**James Lyles Sr. and Chirena Lyles,** thank you for being Sherrod's friend when he needed you. I should have warned you that he was super-kid, huh? You both always welcomed him to visit. You were always loving and protective of what happened around Sherrod. Thank you for loving him the way you did.

**Pete and Cathy Belcher**, you were invaluable on countless occasions by welcoming Sherrod into your home during school hours, when some of those episodes occurred. Only God could have placed the nicest people right near the school. You made your home a safe-haven for our son. You were always available and loved Sherrod as if he were your own. You proved love has no color.

**Mom (Celia) Boyd**, I cannot imagine the pain a grandmother experiences watching her grandchild suffer. You prayed, rubbed his head and held him with long hugs time and time again. Thank you for never giving up and whispering in his ears that God would heal him. He believed you and God did!

**Rovenia "Roe" Braddy,** if it were not for you, this project would still be on the shelf. You were always available for whatever questions I had, and you know I had many. Thank you for your guidance and expertise.

**Donna Barber,** you provided a keen eye with your reading skills after our eyes became blind to the edits you found. Thank you for helping this project along at a very critical time in its development.

**Shawn West** (our first born), you were the great big brother for Sherrod. You never questioned why your brother received all the attention during some of your most formative years. You sacrificed a great deal. Despite not having your dad to bounce life off at times, you found a way to succeed in silence. Thank you for understanding at a young age the plight of your family. You did an awesome job supporting your Mom and Dad and protecting your brother. You have always been a giver. God has given you many gifts. I pray you use them all. The world deserves to benefit from what happens when you walk in the room. I love you.

**Sherrod West** "Rod", much of what you will read here you may or may not remember. The nine years you endured this disorder can only be summed up with one word, remarkable! You taught your dad so much about life during those times. Thank you for encouraging the entire family when you needed encouragement yourself. God selected you for this assignment and you helped put your family back together. You answered the call and made Him and us proud. You had questions but you never complained. You were a warrior which is what makes you the warrior you are today. God has planted a seed in you, one that should remind you that you can do all things through Christ who gives you strength (Phil

4:13).  Never forget what God did in you and always tell your story.  I love you.

**Our Community of Believers,** to all the prayer warriors that know our story.  If I missed you above, please charge it to my head and not my heart.  I want to thank you for continually praying and encouraging us along the way.  Your prayers reached God's heart.

**#ourtribe**

# FORWARD

As the founder and Sr. Pastor of DaySpring Ministries for thirty years and the Founder and President of the Mighty Men of Valor (MVM), National Men's Conference for twenty years, I want to acknowledge and congratulate Wink as an early disciple of my work. I'm very proud to witness his courage and transparency in letting his scars speak in his book, "From Dusk til Dawn." Wink's book is a reminder of what God desires all of us to do when BLINDSIDED. Trust in Jesus with all our heart so when the battle is over you can testify about His love and protection. Wink didn't wait until the battle was over. He shouted along the way and forged his test into a powerful testimony by "letting our scars speak." The best way to see God in any hardship is by not giving up, facing your challenges, and enduring until the end in the power of the Holy Spirit. Leave the results to God. Trouble, trials, and hardships are God's way of building our faith in Him while bringing out the best in us. This book clearly shows Wink as a man who has been stretched, tested, and stayed the course until his test resulted in this book...his written testimony. This is proof that God will never leave or forsake us and that victory is assured. Wink has become a champion and part of a cloud of witnesses for faith. Jesus assured us that greater is HE that is in us than he that is in the world. God's way of proving this is to create a situation(s) that requires more than we humanly think we can handle and then inserts us into it.

Many of these trials feel like they are more than we can handle. That's the point... it is more than we can handle in our own strength. God ensures that the hedge of protection also serves as a barrier to keep us in. This prevents us from getting out prematurely, before His will is accomplished (Job 3:23-25 NIV).

God shows Himself by sending us HELP...people; (Exodus 17:12 NKJV) "But Moses' hands became heavy; so, they took a stone and put it under him, and he sat on it. And Aaron and Hur supported his hands, one on one side, and the other on the other side; and his hands were steady until the going down of the sun." Wink shows us that the power that works within us (Holy Spirit), coupled with the support the people in our lives gives us, helps us endure until we achieve victory.

You may not have to face Wink and his family's trial but be assured, you will face trials/trouble daily (Matthew 6:34 NIV), "Therefore, do not worry about tomorrow, for tomorrow will worry about itself." Each day has enough trouble of its own.

Wink shows us how to accept our designer trial as gifts from God and to look to the hills from where our help comes from.

God has created a platform and a way for him to express the love of God as a dynamic praise warrior!   Hardships produce awesome worship. Write-on/Right-on Wink!

**Dr. Cliff Ashe III**

# PREFACE

It is by the grace of God that we live, move, and have purpose for our being. It is our prayer that the contents of this book will bring truth to a world in which many who don't know or have forgotten who God is. It is also our prayer that the words that you read will encourage your heart to come to know that it is He (God) that makes all things well.

The family as I know it has become increasingly extinct in our society. With some statistics reporting the divorce rate is climbing to over 60 percent, men are leaving their headship as husbands and fathers, and are following selfish goals. You might ask, "Why this book at this time?" I'm glad you asked that question! It all started with a prayer. It was 1997 and our family was not in a good place at all. I had done such a poor job leading my family that it seemed as though the best alternative was to call it quits and move on with life. God had blessed me with a great family. My wife Ann was an accomplished teacher of seventeen years at that time. We had been married for nearly sixteen years and were blessed to have two great young mighty men - Shawn, then 13, and Sherrod, 8. We were a military family, so we moved around quite a bit, with our last assignment being in Pennsylvania. Not only did this denote the ending of a very successful military career, but it also became the start of the ending of another thing, me and my wife's marriage. It seems anything that required a negotiation brought division between the entire family and me. I don't know why I ever assumed this was a fair draw, but nevertheless, I took on the challenge every time, with hopes of coming out on top. I loved my family, but I didn't like them very much. I felt as though they had established a unified front just to take me out. They did not like me very much either. I was known as the raging tyrant. I didn't understand then that it was my lack of leadership that caused the division. The remarkable thing is the fact that I knew a great deal about leadership from my military background but did not apply much of it to my life at home.

Ann and I were childhood sweethearts with deep Christian foundations. We were both Christ followers. My mother, who is deceased, laid the foundation and taught me the truths of the Word of God at an early age. She was the greatest example and influence of a Christ-centered life that I have ever known. Ann also grew up in a Christian home, and we both attended the same church as teens. The one thing that kept me from making one of the worst decisions I could have ever made with a divorce, was the memory of what it was like not having a father around for the first eight years of my life. I remember Mom juggling both mother and father roles, trying to make ends meet. At that time, it was my younger multi-talented brother and me. Mom did a wonderful job raising us until receiving help when she married my stepdad. I called him Pop. He was the first consistent positive male influence in my life. He possessed God-given leadership skills and street smarts that made young people want to be around him. Prior to, and especially after Pop intersected my life, I had always promised myself that if I ever married and had children, I would never abandon them. This promise came from deep convictions of a biological father that was always around, but never present in my life. But here I was about to renege on that promise to God and myself. The thought of going through with divorce always haunted me. Thus was the prayer that changed my life. Although I don't remember my exact words, it went something like this: "Lord I tried, but it just ain't working. We don't even like each other and I can't do this anymore! If we don't get help, we are not going make it."

I remember something Mom would often say to me after I would escape danger from doing things that she believed dishonored God. She would say things like, "Wink, God must really love you!" I thought she was referring to God letting me get away with a lot without passing judgment or something. She wasn't referring to that at all. She was trying to get me to understand just how much God loved everyone! I thought I was special. I thought I was God's friend and that He looked out for me because Mom asked Him to do so. I believe Mom must have thought that about everyone. During her home-going service where thousands attended, I heard many say that she had either treated or told them they were special. They quickly discovered that everyone she interacted with was special to her, and they had all showed up to pay their respects in the same place at the same time. I think some were disappointed to discover that. So, it is with God. We are all special.

I thought Mom's prayers for God to cover me meant don't hurt him. I have come to learn that when you have praying parents, God honors those prayers, even after they are gone. Isn't that amazing?! It's incomprehensible for my understanding that God would honor prayers even after one has passed from this life. I had no idea that Mom's prayers were being answered even after her death. It definitely didn't look like prayers were being answered, but they were. Amid a broken family and marriage, something else happened that surely should have been the nail in the coffin. God allowed our family to experience yet another blow that only He could rescue us from. We were stricken with a health diagnosis that ignited my prayer.

The way our lives were going, I didn't think anybody was praying about anything the right way. When Ann and I prayed as young adults for God to bless our lives as we started one together, we had no idea that God would honor that prayer even when we would rather He ignore our request. We had no idea how much He really did love us. In the turning of the pages to follow, you will find out how much He really did and does love us all. He showed us just how much He loves us when He sent His son to a cross.

We pray that what you read will remind you of His unfailing love for you. He has not forgotten you. As a matter of fact, He was with you yesterday, today and will be with you tomorrow! Never lose hope in the promises in God's Word. As God told Joshua, He is telling you, He will never leave you or forsake you (Joshua 1:5). It is our witness, when you are in the darkest of a storm, when your faith is shaken to the very core, and there seems to be no way out, we know without question, morning is coming. After night has cast its shadow over the sun, the Son still shines! God is that parent bidding their child to take that next step. He is right there standing with us in the shadows of death moving us all into the marvelous light.

We want to thank you for taking the time to go on a journey with one family's plight of brokenness and a health crisis.

Life throws us all blows, and some of them can be hard to handle.

Our blow came at a time that our family would agree was a heavy one. It's a journey through a period that only we can share. You have one to share as well, we all do.

In His Grip,

Wink West

# Chapter 1

## In The Beginning

This was the summer of 1997. After planning our summer vacation earlier in the year, I was ready to go, hurrying the family to get into the car. I confess, once I have something planned when it's time to execute, I have very little patience in or with waiting. The boys, then 13 and 8 were trying to pack everything they could to complement the drive and their hotel room. My wife Ann was finishing making sandwiches for our trip to Busch Gardens, VA. We packed the cold cut sandwiches wrapped in aluminum foil with a ton of mayo on them, a big jumbo bag of Lay's Potato Chips and to top it all off, the Tastykake krimpets and of course red Kool-Aid on ice. We were ready to go! As I recall, it was a hot sunny day trip and anyone who knows the Washington D.C. Beltway area also knows that it's a stop and start journey, with mostly stops when you reach that area.

We arrived five hours later, checked into our hotel and began to plan the events for the next five days of our vacation. This area of Virginia, although beautiful as it could be with the cherry blossom trees, presented problems for sinuses. Early into the vacation, Sherrod started complaining that his eyes were itching and began blinking quite a bit. No one else in the family was bothered so we associated the symptoms with possible allergies. We went to the local drug store to get allergy eye drops to help relieve the itching and to help control the very noticeable blinking. Although he was blinking quite a bit, he did not let that interfere with the fun. Kids will never let fun get interrupted; oh no! Even though we believed the boys were having a good time, we were concerned that Sherrod might not have been enjoying himself as much as we had hoped. He reassured us that absolutely nothing got in the way of his fun. I should have known that nothing gets in the way of any kid that is in the fun zone. Arms could be falling off, but the fun will go on.

The summer ended, and the boys returned to school. Ann also returned to school as a teacher, as she had done in past years. I had been retired from the military just two years and had found work with a very well-known electrical distribution center. Although the work had nothing to do with my administrative background, it yielded the best pay at the time, and as I had wished, kept me away from paperwork. The end of this summer would begin a journey for our family that anyone would only hope was a bad dream that would soon end. We would soon discover that this was not a dream at all. It would become a real-life tsunami storm, allowed by God, for the right family, at the right time.

I remember when we first received the diagnosis about Sherrod's health challenge. The information we received became overwhelming. We were presented with various reports that sounded very scary. At first, we hoped it was just a bad reaction to something but as the doctors conversed, we would be handed a diagnosis of something called Tourette syndrome (T.S.). We had no idea what it was, but the name didn't sound good at all. Although we didn't know anything about T.S., our smiles quickly turned to frowns hearing about its affects. It was as if someone had given our family a shot to the gut and we were just trying to catch our breath. Instead of acknowledging that we were out right scared and uninformed, we did like so many others and smiled for the bright lights and cameras while hurting on the inside.

Initially, after receiving the report, I processed the information personally. In my head I remember saying, "What if I'm possibly responsible?" Why was I wearing guilt? (1) I knew my walk with Christ was less than authentic and (2) my leadership as a husband

and father was failing. I knew God wanted to do more with and in me than I was allowing Him to do. I was running away from what God had planned for me and I started to feed my flesh with boyish behavior, dabbling with illegal drugs which led to my life unraveling in so many other ways. I believed the things that were going on with Sherrod could possibly be a direct reflection of my walk.

It was just one of those after thoughts. I was dealing with some heavy guilt about my own life that drove me to believe that it was me that caused the crippling effects that T.S had on my son. Ann on the other hand looked at me hoping I had answers. Our marriage was in trouble, but I was still her hero. I could see the helplessness in her eyes and the sadness in her face. I usually have answers for everything, but not this time. My eyes welded up as they met hers. I gave her a long hug to let her know we were in this together. There were many nights we cried like a choir in harmony.  As I look back at that time, we were seen as such a perfect little family by so many, that we were afraid to let others know we were in a crisis and had issues just like everyone else.  This would be a process of learning and growing we knew little about, so we hid as much as we could for as long as we could.  We missed the value in accepting and embracing the process, believing that if we didn't acknowledge or just ignored them, our problems would somehow go away.

This became somewhat like a tangled web in the sense that we were already hiding the real condition of the family prior to this news.  The news only put our family on the front page of a story called life.

To add some clarity to what I'm referencing, there are a couple of things that we need to understand when going through any life crisis.

# 1. Acknowledgment

Acknowledge everything about your issue or crisis to trusted individuals. That means the good and the bad. This is very important, and I would say critical that you acknowledge:

a. That your issue or crisis is bigger than you

b. That you can't fix it

c. That you need help.

If you have decided to ask almighty God to intervene, there is a warning label that comes with that request. That warning label reads, "I am a sovereign God. I specialize in your case. I will fix it my way and for your good if you remain in me, guaranteed." I understand this is a conjecture, but that's just God's nature. He does what He wants how He wants as He answers your prayer. He places this warning label on every case He decides to take. We don't get to choose how He gets us there, but He guarantees His work if we abide in Him (Jn 15:4).

Many of us won't acknowledge that we are broken, confused and frustrated, and ready to give up. If you don't have someone that you can <u>trust</u> to acknowledge these things, you will more than likely start masking your condition and deepen your struggle.

## 2. Talk through the journey

It helps to have someone to talk to about the feelings that come and go while or when going through a crisis. We all go through various feelings when going through a life challenge. Some days you are doing well and other days you are at your wit's end.

I'm not even sure our family was in the right space to invite anyone into this part of our world at that time. This would mean opening not only the doors of our home to others, but also opening the doors of our hearts to others. This would be an invitation into the pain and struggles we would experience along the way and the ones we ignored.

Those feelings were pretty raw at first, and everything was so new that we didn't quite know how to process it all ourselves. It's almost like what Ann used to tell me about the announcement of her being pregnant. She would say, "I don't want to tell people too early on. It makes the pregnancy seem longer." I think that's a nice way to say, she didn't want people asking her questions about her pregnancy every time she saw them, so she wanted to wait awhile. Our thinking about Sherrod having T.S. was along those lines. The sooner we tell people, the sooner we would get questions and the sooner our little perfectly looking lives would be invaded and exposed. It's pretty hard to smile for the bright lights and cameras consistently when going through a challenging time. Once others know your true status, it's only their duty to bug you about it often. I used the word "bug" because of how it feels, not that those feelings are accurate. Others are concerned and don't want you to think you are forgotten. The many friends and family members that become aware of your crisis feel the need to come to your rescue. Although our circumstances and challenges in life may not be yours, we all have them.

Our prayer is that something that we share about our experience will bless you as you walk out yours. We expect God to move on your behalf. Why? Because He did it for us! Like I previously said, it all started with a prayer. Oh, so maybe after reading these few pages you are contemplating maybe not praying so much? That is not a good decision. The Bible declares in James 5:16 that the prayers you pray, if prayed with a sincere heart produce awesome results, so keep on praying and don't stop! If you keep reading you will discover one family's plight and fulfillment of a promise as a result of a sincere prayer.

## Outtake

If God allowed each of us to choose our own challenges in life, I would guess we would all choose the type that would keep us away from that perfect fellowship He intended us to have with Him.  God knows this and loves us just that much.  The Bible says He determined if we were going to come to know and love Him in all His glory, there would have to be an immoveable force that would draw us straight to Him.  He uses this type of method throughout the Bible as well as in our lives today.  That immoveable force creates the need to call on a God that responds in ways that are beyond our understanding, but for our good.

I had no idea that the very thing I was praying not to happen was the very thing that needed to happen.  The answer to my prayer was wrapped up in our test!  God knew that in order for Him to heal my marriage it needed to be at a breaking point.  He needed to bring the very thing I dreaded with a divorce to help Ann and I understand the purpose He put us together in the first place. God had a plan for us before we were born. He purposed that we would glorify Him in our marriage and we needed an opportunity to see, hear and feel how important we were to each other in the marriage. There needed to be an obstacle bigger than us that would move us closer to Him and each other. So God provided a test in the form of a health crisis to bring out the best He put in us. Each of us has a "best" just waiting to come out. Most times we see the best people have to offer when it's called out of them. Called out is another way of saying forced out. We see it in sports and in life. One team rises to a level above its opponent. A supervisor challenges an employee about their work performance and the employee makes remarkable improvements. Our best was being forced out.

It was also a test to determine our level of dependency on ourselves and how much we depended on and trusted in God. As we strive to overcome each new challenge, God gives us assurance and hope each and every time that He is with us (Matt 28:20). It becomes a trust factor. The circumstances that gripped our family taught us what trusting in God really means. It means that you don't have to understand how your situation will turn around, but you trust that it will. It means that you don't have to have all the answers to the questions others ask about your situation, but you trust that the answers will come. It means that you have the assurance that God has your best interest in mind. We needed to keep our eyes on Him and not on our situation. When the waves of life get really strong, I have learned that my trust in God should remind me that the One who calms the seas will also calm my situation.

I understand that what you are reading about trust may sound pretty practical in theory, but the reality is it's much harder to practice. This is why it's so important to tell your story. It helps others that may have lost hope. Tell the entire story. The parts that are the hardest to tell and hurt the most are the parts that heal the deepest. There is someone waiting to hear what you have to say about the life they are living. Yes, you need to speak into someone else's life by telling them about your own. Someone's life may be in the balance waiting on the story you have to tell. A story does no one any good if it goes to the grave untold. If our story helps you, your story may help someone else and if that is reciprocal, we are all helped and we are all healed. As I said earlier, it's easier said and harder done. If more of us would tell our stories, so many more would be free from many of life's challenges.

It starts with you and your story. God is writing one just for you to tell. At the end of the day, if your story isn't told, someone may have lost hope that could have been saved. This one is being shared for that very reason. We want you to know that there is hope. We want readers to hear about our trials and our triumphs because we truly believe both provide lessons. Always be prepared to give an answer to everyone who asks you to give the reason for the hope that you have. (1 Pet 3:15)

# Chapter 2

## Who's to Blame?

I really didn't want to believe my son's illness was my fault, but I couldn't shake the thought that it just may be my fault and if it were, how would I ever forgive myself for any contribution I may have made. I thought I could somehow negotiate my way back to God and turn my life around if He would first rescue my son from the grip of his illness. I know that may not have been very smart, right? I was desperate.

Here was our family, with an 8-year-old who was completely healthy (so we thought) and then a bomb was dropped right in the middle of our lives. T.S. invaded our space and decided it wanted to reside. Prior to the family discovering this disorder, we had received reports from our son's third grade teacher that he was leaving used tissues in his desk. We were also finding tissue particles in the family's washing machine left in his pants pockets. Not knowing what was going on, we instructed him to stop leaving tissues in his desk and in his pants pockets. After all, he didn't show signs of a cold or even any rubbing of the eyes, so in our minds, there was no need for him to carry tissues around. Sherrod did not have or share an answer for why he was carrying these tissues, so we expected him to comply with our wishes. To our surprise, the tissues kept showing up both in his desk and in his pants. He knew the consequences for disobedience, so we assumed either he had lost his mind by being disobedient or there must be a deeper issue. After having a serious conversation with Sherrod, we discovered he was carrying the tissues around to muffle a sound he could not control. We sought help at our local military health clinic. That appointment led us to a specialist at Hershey Medical Center. After a series of tests, we discovered the early signs of his T.S. first manifested in the form of blinking and now as a verbal sound called tics. This was the sound he would try to muffle with tissues.

The specialist told us that Sherrod had a very mild case of the disorder. Although that report was soothing, we had never even heard of T.S. so our hopes were that it would be something temporary.

The vocal tics became stronger and stronger by the days and weeks to the point that neighbors could hear him clear down the street from a closed bedroom door. His throat and chest would ache from hours of outbursts. To add to the outbursts, he began losing control of his body. One moment he would be standing and the next picking himself off the floor from an involuntary muscle spasm of some sort. It would bring tears to his and our eyes. He pleaded for Ann and I to get him some relief. Those pleas led us to repeated visits to the local hospital emergency room. The hospital would give us sedatives to help calm him, which seemed to help at one point. Going to the emergency room became a normal occurrence. The hospital would treat him with sedatives and send us on our way. Although giving us some relief, at times the sedatives were turning our son into a zombie. Yes, we did need some relief for sure, but the drugs were a bit much for a child.

It seemed right at dusk the episodes would begin and continue through the entire evening into early morning. It was almost like clockwork. Sometimes, we would be up so late/early that it was almost impossible for the family to function at work or school later that morning.

The journey began as we searched for answers to why this was happening to our family. At the same time, our son had become more interested in our welfare more so than his own. There were times, as he laid on the hospital gurney, he would look us in the eyes and reassure Ann and I that it was going to be okay. Out of his own pain and struggles he would tell us he was sorry for what we had to endure. Little did he know that his acceptance for and about his plight with T.S. was a building block for his family's acceptance and courage to move forward with whatever God had in store.

We wanted Sherrod healed and we wanted him to receive the best treatment possible. One of my prayers was if God would just put us in the presence of a doctor from John's Hopkins Hospital in Baltimore, MD, that would be the answer to our problem. For those of you who don't know about John's Hopkins, this hospital produces some of the top doctors in the country and since we lived approximately two hours away, if it were available, I wanted our son to receive help from the best.

To show you how much God loves us and cares about his children, we didn't even have to go to John's Hopkins; John's Hopkins came to us! Let me explain. As you may recall, we were a military family. The best hospital in our area for the military was Walter Reed Army Medical Center in Washington, D.C. Just so you can get a picture of how advanced they were with audio and video technologies back in the 90's, we were able to video teleconference with Walter Reed from the Army's Health Clinic in Pennsylvania. Today we call that Face Time, back then it was called *amazing*. Our son made a good connection with the doctor on the screen. From that consultation, we scheduled an appointment to make an in-person visit. Anxious to get help, the family scheduled and made our way to Walter Reed with documentation and footage to show what was going on in our home almost every evening. The footage captured was difficult to record as well as watch. It was heart wrenching having to film my son struggle in the middle of the night trying to fight off T.S's torment. It showed some of the involuntary movements Sherrod had to endure during some of those dreadful nights. We had great expectations about the trip because we were being hopeful that some expert would figure this all out and we would be on our way home and live happily ever after.

I remember driving onto the hospital property, Sherrod was half asleep but there were signs of his T.S. slightly flaring up. During the drive up, I would occasionally look back in the rear-view mirror and see his little body contort while he tried to sleep. It was perfect timing because the doctors needed to see what was going on with his body with their own eyes. But just in case they didn't get to see anything, we had a video. We wanted so badly to make this moment count. The receptionist on the neurological disorders floor asked us to sit for a few moments in a waiting area. Not long after, we were called into the doctor's office and told to have another seat, and that the doctor would be right in. Minutes went by. Ann was scanning the room and so was I. Sherrod was trying to contain his body movements. I reminded him that it was okay to relax; the doctor would understand. In walked a tall, slim Caucasian gentlemen wearing a long white jacket, tan Dockers and a stethoscope around his neck. He seemed to be in his mid 30's and had a unique way of carrying himself. Some would say he had what they call *swag*. He walked over and put his hand out first to greet Sherrod. Then he greeted us. That was a great second impression for Sherrod because the doctor made him feel as though he was top priority. We sat and spoke with the doctor. To be honest, it was mostly the doctor and Sherrod having a conversation and we just happened to be in the room. The doctor could see Sherrod's T.S. flaring up as he banged his foot on the floor, making a loud thunderous sound, and shook his head violently from left to right. He seemed embarrassed, but the doctor told him that it was perfectly fine, and that they were going to get him some help. Sherrod immediately looked up at Ann and me and started smiling. His eyes seem to be saying, "It's going to be over soon Dad and Mom; we are going to get help." I smiled back at him and rubbed his head to communicate that I agreed with him. Ann just smiled and nodded her head in agreement as well. Then I looked up at the wall which captured the doctor's credentials. I could not believe my eyes, but there it was. I saw a medical degree from the one and only John's Hopkins University Medical School! I thought, "You have got to be kidding me!" I tapped Ann on the shoulder as she listened intently to the doctor talk through procedures he wanted to try. I interrupted him by pointing to the certificate on the wall. He stopped talking and looked in the direction I was pointing. Ann looked over at me and smiled, but I don't think she was as impressed as I was, because it was my prayer that God would allow us to see someone from John's Hopkins. She was more interested and focused on the type of help our son would receive. The doctor explained that after having an opportunity to observe Sherrod in person, he believed he had a medication that might help, but unfortunately offered no cure for Sherrod's condition. We were grateful for the help we were receiving, but to be honest, I had high expectations after I believed God had answered my prayer, but he only offered assistance to help Sherrod manage his disorder. We all left that office in good spirits believing we were turning the corner and God was finally giving us at least some help. We received some medication and encouragement from the doctor and went on our way back home.

After a few days of having the new medication in his system, Sherrod's episodes died down quite a bit. We were so happy for some relief for him, and to be honest, for us too. The meds were working!

It would be weeks later and after a couple of visits and telephone conference calls it was determined that the medicine wasn't working as well as we had thought. It was back to the drawing board, and we were getting a little discouraged. Yes, we were getting discouraged like many others do. We believed our plans for Sherrod's healing were almost perfect. At least I believed with all my heart God had answered our prayer. Why would God give us the best only to find out they couldn't help? When plans fail, discouragement comes. I thought having a doctor from one of the most prestigious hospitals in the country would fix our problem, but it didn't.

Sometimes God will allow you to have exactly what you ask for just to show you that it isn't what you need, or better yet, that what you receive isn't going to get you the results you seek. Our plans needed to fail so that God's plans could be recognized and acknowledged. God was moving my plans out of the way in order to usher in His own.

## Outtake

As I recalled the emotional rollercoaster in this chapter, I'm reminded of what happens when we experience the highs and lows of life. It doesn't matter if you are a Christ follower or not, we all have emotions and feelings. We tried to deliver our story in a way for you to see the raw emotions we felt when we heard the news of Sherrod's condition, and also the condition of our lives. As you read the chapter, there is a shift in my emotions from what I prayed and what God was doing to answer that prayer. Sometimes, the focus of the issue you face needs to shift so that it's placed where it should be. My initial focus in my prayer was my marriage and God saw fit to change my focus to save my marriage. Isaiah 55: 8-9 says "8 My thoughts are nothing like your thoughts," says the LORD. And my ways are far beyond anything you could imagine. 9 For just as the heavens are higher than the earth, so my ways are higher than your ways and my thoughts higher than your thoughts." God was answering my prayer His way and in His time.

There was a saying my pastor, Dr. Cliff Ashe, used to quote years ago. He would say, "sin will take you further than you want to go, keep you longer than you want to stay and cost you more than you ever wanted to pay". The guilt sin leaves screams so much louder than the temporary pleasure it brings. Sin was ringing in my ears.

During the early part of this story, my life was a mess. I recall Mom reminding me on countless occasions that God answers her prayers. Actually, I almost incorporated a chapter called "Cursed by a Prayer". The meaning was to try to articulate the power of prayer. I wanted readers to know that God really does honor the prayers of the righteous. I believed my Mom was one of the righteous and because I believed her, I also believed that when she prayed God heard her. This is the reason I rarely asked Mom to pray for me.

I know now that many who have had loved ones pray for them more than likely experienced the rod of correction as a result of prayer. I also knew as a young man, my issues and sins were young. As I became a man, my issues became larger and so did my sins. I developed an understanding with my mind of God's possible reaction to prayer, but my heart never comprehended the eternal provision of prayer. I didn't know that some of those prayers were signed off by Mom saying things like, "whatever be your will for his life, bring him in alignment with it God". "If you have to break him to make him God, do it." I now realize she trusted God so much that she would say ridiculous things. Hold on now, why do I need to be broken to get the message? That is exactly the point! God usually has to break up something in us in order to put us back together the right way.

In my desperation to have my prayer answered, I learned God answered everything I requested in this chapter just to move my wants and wishes off the table to point me to Himself. It was as if God was trying to help me see that I didn't even know what I should pray. I'm so glad He did it His way because if my prayer would have ended with God saying "I gave you everything you asked for", my life would still be a mess. Why? I was asking God to fix my situation, not my life.

I have no idea what you may be praying about and why you are praying. Hear this. If you love God and you believe He loves you, He hears you! (Jn 5:14). When you can't understand His ways, remember what you know about Him. Trust His character. He took our family on a trip called *straight* in an around about way. His way! I often tell my friends that when we pray and ask God to come in and handle certain situations, God usually starts working on the requestor. Another interesting thought is that God also usually handles an array of issues surrounding your request. That's just how powerful our God is! He can answer multiple prayers and solve them all with one solution. Do you remember reading about the prayer I had about my family? I had no idea God was going to answer my prayer starting with me. Actually, it started with a prayer from Mom to Him to guide me into all truth. Mom talked too much! Maybe you have or need someone in your life that talks to God too much.

# Chapter 3

## The Search

Here we were in the middle of a life crisis, seemingly with no one to turn to and nowhere to go. All the doctors we sought really could not come up with the right solution to the problem. Although some of the things they prescribed helped for a short period of time, his symptoms would return with a vengeance and would heighten to another level. We started experiencing him doing things that could either hurt himself or those around him. He would lose control of his body and begin flailing his arms and legs. He could be in the middle of dinner and have one of his involuntary muscle spasms and lose control of the fork in his hand. Before you knew it, the fork would fly from his hand clear across the room. Other times he would stomp his foot very hard on the floor because his legs would decide that's what they wanted to do. On top of that, his vocal tics had reached an all-time high. This left him with a sore throat and neighbors thinking there was a fight going on at the West Residence.

We concluded the reason everything happened during the early evening hours into early morning was because Sherrod suppressed all the symptoms in throughout the day while attending school. Home was a safe environment for him to let it all out, and out they came! Again, back and forth to the emergency rooms we would go. There were times you could see the helplessness on hospital attendants faces as they politely suggested the sedatives so that the family could get some rest. This was the cycle we would face much too often. As we covered acknowledgement in a previous chapter, a relative to acknowledgement is acceptance. We had to accept first to ourselves, then to family, friends and the school system that there was a health issue facing our family and it was called T.S.

To show the progression of Sherrod's disorder, we went from a child in 2nd grade trying to get through his day by muffling sounds he couldn't control with tissues, to a middle school student on prescribed medication. There were days the medicine would fail, and I would receive a call from the school letting me know that I needed to come to the counselor's office to collect my son because his disorder had gotten out of control. I remember some of those calls. I used the word "collect" because there were times when I was doing exactly that, picking my son up off the floor because of an episode that left him helpless.

It was amazing that Sherrod could even function at all during the day, knowing he was operating off very little sleep from being up most of the night prior. Actually, there were times he did end up back home just because he could not stay awake in class. As with most mornings Ann and I would have prayer with both boys for their protection, but especially for God to protect Sherrod and help him not feel ashamed or embarrassed if he would have an episode while in the presence of his school mates. Times were tough then. As I mentioned, the family was operating on sheer will to get through the day from being exhausted.

One saving grace for our oldest Shawn was that he was active and hanging out with his high school friends, which I'm sure helped him take his mind off of things going on at home. He and his friends would meet at the youth center and at each other's homes but rarely at ours. He didn't have a problem inviting friends over, but not inviting them to the house was his way of protecting his younger brother from embarrassment. He was shielding the entire family and being big brother at the same time. He understood that right around dusk, was a signal to be on guard. It was as if dusk was a trigger for Sherrod's T.S. to flare up in and of itself.

Each day we would brace ourselves for what was to come. I often wondered how Shawn must have felt not being able to assist his little brother, especially since he was the first one to notice the signs before anyone else. He never asked why or behaved as if he thought we didn't think he was important. He was a great example of a child who knew instinctively that his brother needed our attention a little more and he just wanted to stay out of the way. He was so good at not being in the way that we often asked each other of his whereabouts. I also think he didn't really want to experience watching his little brother's transformation each night. It was a lot for a young teen to witness.

If I was ever away from the home when Sherrod's episodes kicked in, I would be immediately summoned back. If I was out of town, I would call trusted friends, like Mr. Walter Butler who was 20 miles away, to go by and assist Ann with *super-kid* because he was just too strong for her to handle alone. I would joke around with him to make light of some of the heaviness we were experiencing. I would recount some of the episodes with him and add my embellishments about his strength of course. He would respond embarrassingly as if to say, "stop Dad, let it go." Since his episodes caused him to fall, we would encourage him to stay on the floor once he was there to prevent him from hurting himself. Not that being on the floor was much better because something about the medicine he was taking mixed with his condition made him turn into what I labeled *super-kid*. He was a super-kid in the sense that he could levitate from the floor from lying on his back. He could spring up approximately three feet in the air and back down again. Please do not ask me how this is possible because I have no idea. All I know is it happened on many occasions. I would press him to the floor and at times place a mattress on the floor under him to soften his landings and prevent a fall on his head. This could go on for most of the night, and it did most nights, until we discovered that a ride in the car would work miracles. Yes, a ride in the car! It was actually a van at the time. I believe it began just to give him air because his episodes were like a good workout for sure, leaving him exhausted. Well, he may have needed air, but I needed air too! Hello! I was working hard trying to prevent him from hurting himself, his family, and from breaking stuff around the house. Some of those items were from Germany and were valuable to us. We would struggle to get him into the van. But once he was there, off he and I would go. Initially, it was like a continuation of what was going on in the house, with him kicking the doors and his body being thrown from here to there. As we would make our way down the road and onto the interstate, he would slowly but surely start to settle down. He would begin to thank me for taking him out and taking care of him. Essentially, he was thanking me for just being his dad. Wow! Those were some special moments. I would look over at him, while keeping one eye on the road, and thank God for just allowing his body to relax for a moment. Then he would start to get sleepy approximately 20 minutes into the ride. With a slur in his voice, he would ask me to put on some jazz or classical music from the radio. I asked why that type of music and he would tell me he just wanted to hear soft music without singing. I would scroll through the radio stations until he heard something that he liked. Once I landed on something he liked, I could see his body settle into a more relaxed position. We have a very dear friend who is a gospel recording artist, who has a jazz-like style voice. Sherrod would ask to hear her music at times. She sang on her CD but that was the only music he requested besides traditional or contemporary jazz or classical music. She was humbled to hear how her music was serving our family.

He would say short sentences, half asleep, expressing how he was feeling in that moment. The conversations were brief but powerful. I sure wish I could have recorded some of those talks. As best I can recall, they went something like this:

Sherrod: "Hey dad, thank you for doing all you are doing for me."

Wink: "No problem, son. It's going to be alright. God is going to heal you, Rod." (Rod was the nickname I called him.)

Sherrod: "I know; it's okay though, Dad."

What he was basically telling me was if God didn't heal him, he was going to accept that. It took everything within me to keep it together after hearing him say that. As much as I wanted to rescue him from all he was going through, there was nothing I could do.  Even though I was failing trying to find answers, he was grateful for my efforts.  It only inspired me to do more, whatever *more* was.  Those were sacred father and son moments.  I could say defining moments.  He would then start to doze off into a deeper sleep.

Wherever I was during our travels, I would make my way to a safe turnaround point and start back towards home. On the way back to the house I would have one of those me and God moments.  I would very quietly ask God questions in my head.  I didn't want to disturb Sherrod's sleep or have him see tears coming down my face.  I did not want him to attribute my tears to fear or hopelessness, so I made sure I was as quiet as possible.  It was in those moments that I heard nothing but God's silence to my questions.  I wanted to know why my family had to deal with this health issue.  Why would a nice child like Sherrod have to endure this for his life?  Why did everything we try, from the medicine to the people, fail?  I didn't want anyone in the family to see me in that state.  I was supposed to be the rock of the family. I was the one everyone else looked to for guidance and help.  So, when I had those quiet moments where I could take off my mask, I treasured them.  Those moments helped me breathe.  The only problem I had was God went on break and I was waiting on His return.  While waiting for answers, my frustration would turn into anger because we just didn't know where to turn.  All I wanted was for God to answer us and I felt He was ignoring our cries for help.  It would be because it was for my good and for His glory that He kept silent.

Ann and I had a system in place for our arrival. She would receive a call from me just before my return from our drive and would make sure she had the front door propped open, and his bed covers turned down.  I would lift his limp body from the van and carry him straight to his bed. If you were able to witness me pulling up to the house around two or three in the morning, you would see what I can say was a very smooth operation. Usually by the time his head hit the pillow, it was lights out. Goodnight or good early morning. We would gather a few hours' sleep, and later as always, get together as a family to say our everyday morning prayer followed by a bid for each other to have a great day. I can recall those morning circle prayers and catching a glimpse of some of the family sleeping and not praying. To be honest, we all suffered from insomnia quite a bit because T.S. had kept us up all night. Then I would get in my car and drive to my job praying that I would not receive a call from the school telling me my son was having a bad day and that I needed to come get him.

Throughout those days while at work each time the telephone would ring, I would pray and brace myself before answering the telephone. There was one instance that stands out from many of the calls that I did receive. When I arrived at the school I remember pulling up to the front of the building and from my car I could hear Sherrod's vocal tics. He was in the guidance counselor's office. That office was positioned in the front of the school. As I made my way to that office, the sound of his voice became even more prevalent. I opened the guidance counselor's door and there was my son on the floor surrounded by the guidance counselor and the assistant principal. As he looked up at me his eyes seemed to say "I'm sorry Dad, please help me!" It was a very sad time for both of us. I was saddened because it was obvious to me God had not honored my prayer to help my son regarding keeping him from embarrassment in that environment, and the fact that he was being treated as if he were a wild animal let loose from a cage. He was upset for inadvertently kicking a file cabinet and leaving a dent in one of its drawers. He would frequently apologize for a condition he didn't have control over, and it was hard to hear him thinking his condition was his fault. What was even sadder was that some of his teachers didn't understand or buy into the whole T.S. story. This made it even more stressful for a child who was only trying to have what most of us call a "normal" day. So, on this occasion, I picked him up from the floor and carried him to the car. I remember placing him in the back seat so that he could stretch out. He explained, "they don't believe me, Dad", as tears would flow from his eyes and mine. I would reassure him that I believed him. I would take him to a nearby friend's home where he would stay until the workday ended. Thank God for friends whom we trusted and who loved him. It was so important that Sherrod was comfortable to be himself around them, T.S. and all. They were superb! One was a teacher friend that Ann met in the district whose wife was a stay-at-home educator and super special person. I would take him there whenever he had a challenging day, and she would welcome him with open arms. They would allow him to rest on their sofa until Ann or I picked him up after work. They were a Godsend for sure and a resting place for Sherrod. They were sent by God to look out for us. That's just who they were.

There were times the weight of what we were carrying would become pretty overwhelming. We were just worn out physically, mentally and emotionally. I am so glad God watches over our needs. He reminds us in Psalms 22:24 that He has His eye on us. He reminds us that He has not turned His back on us and is attentive to our cries. Although it may not have felt as though He was answering our prayers, He was, in His way and in His time. Just when I thought we were hopeless, God would send us a rescue. He did say He would never leave us so, He was honoring His word and His character. When we have come to what we believe is our wits end, when we have run out of options and have exhausted ourselves with our own plans, God is ever present.

He was with us in our search for help. Although we had tried several things and fell short, He understood that in all our searching we were really in search of Him.

**Outtake**

The most painful part of this chapter came when I had to respond to the call that my son was on the guidance office floor at the school. At the time my job was approximately 20 miles away from the school. While enroute, I pictured Sherrod being restricted or retained by those that knew very little about his condition. I feared he would possibly get hurt or that someone would hurt him. My heart was beating out of control as I drove at an ungodly speed to get to where he was located. To be honest, we knew very little ourselves so asking others to understand what you barely understood yourself is asking quite a bit.

What strikes me is it seems as though our family started to inform others about Sherrod's condition as a way of coming from behind the wall and trying to gain more support. You would think there would be more understanding than misunderstanding. Well, that was not always the case. What we were experiencing at home was a bit much to believe ourselves if we had not witnessed it. There were nights Ann and I asked each other if what we were seeing and experiencing was real or exaggerated. I can only imagine what others may have been saying and feeling. Sherrod was super sensitive about how others treated him as it related to his condition. He could also feel the energy from someone and tell us if he felt they didn't believe his condition was causing him to do or react certain ways.

Since he spent most of his day away from home, Ann and I had very stressful work days just trying to stay focused on our jobs while trying to be attentive to any alerts that might come from the school. We felt super sad sending our child into an environment where some of the very ones that he looked up to for guidance, support and education, were not what he needed them to be within that environment. I truly believe that some of the loss of confidence he experienced while at school came as a result of some of the educators who doubted his claim.

While the pain of knowing Sherrod was getting some bad vibes, jeers, and disbelief at school, God also gave him a soft and safe place to land. Our friends who were so willing to house him during those hard times was God's way of letting us know that although times may have been hard to handle, He always provided a way of escape (1 Cor 10:13). He knows exactly what you need. Where there were bad vibes, we also found those who showed love. Where there were jeers there were others who showed support and where there was disbelief some reassured Sherrod and us they believed everything he said. God sent us refuge.

My hope is to draw an understanding about how I was feeling during the process of God changing my heart while he was changing our circumstance. As I stated in this chapter, I felt God ignored my prayer to keep my son from embarrassment in school. What I now realize is God wasn't trying to embarrass Sherrod at all. He was using him to bring awareness about T.S. to an environment where his condition was basically unknown. Someone needed to be a pioneer and God chose him. He was the right child with the right heart. I truly believe that if God calls you to something He also prepares you for the journey. Some of the preparation comes with blood, sweat and tears and others come with no road map. It doesn't matter how the journey starts, what really matters is how it ends. The Bible tells us that the ending of something is much better than the beginning (Eccl 7:8). It's true on many levels. I have never heard anyone say after only watching the beginning of a movie that it was great. That assessment can only be made at the completion of the full viewing. God is forever writing the script of our lives. There are a few twists and turns that are unexpected but don't be alarmed. Keep your focus with the end in mind.

You may experience a life changing event along the way as we did. There have been very few moments as special as the ride in the car when I couldn't say a word, but God heard my heart and God didn't say a word, but I felt His.

# Chapter 4

## Still Searching

There was one period when Sherrod was around 11 years old where he would try to take off and run. I'm not sure what was happening in his mind, but it seemed as though something was telling him just to get away. Some may say, I think that all the time! Southwest Airlines has a tag line for their marketing with that phrase. Everybody wants to get away, Wink! I get it, me too. At the age of 11 the only getaway place for him was where his feet carried him. This was a very new phase, but a dangerous one as well. This would happen during some of those same early evening hours. He would take off out of the front door (or any door) of the house and run down the street as if he was in a 50-yard dash. At the time, he was already one of the fastest in his school, and I was in pretty good shape myself, but I soon discovered I was no match. What was scary is that our street had very little overhead lighting. On one particular evening, he ran out the front door and tore down the street. I ran after him and approached where I assumed he had run and called his name trying to locate him. As I walked after running a bit, I continued to call his name. It was pitch-black dark in that part of our block. As I walked down the middle of the street trying to ensure I wasn't walking into anything, there he was quietly planted in the middle of the street sitting with his knees in his chest and his head in his lap, rocking back and forth. I picked him up and carried him back to the house.

Running for the front door became an often occurrence that he tried, until Ann and I decided that we needed to fortify the house. When dusk came, we would place the house on lockdown. This meant, locking the doors, removing all sharp items from view and making sure the guards – Ann and I – were on duty.

Things started to rapidly get worse as time went on. We had read about some of the effects of T.S., but what we were experiencing seemed over the top. Doctors had no answers for our questions. Why was Sherrod telling me he was having urges to run? Why would he run down the street with no clothes on and sit in the middle of the road? Why would he pull on the handle of a moving car as if he were going to jump out?

Some of the answers we received from professionals and novices were statements like "he may just want attention" or "I think he is exaggerating his condition a bit." To be totally honest, as we stated earlier, there were times our entire family felt the same way.

Emotionally, the frustration Sherrod must have felt trying to convince everyone that he was not exaggerating his condition is beyond me. At times this frustration would trigger his neurological disorder to heighten where he would shake his head back and forth like rockers do in a rock band and stomp repeatedly. These were some very dark times for us. And to make matters worse, out of nowhere, he began having urges to bite. This was another level of concern altogether. It was especially concerning because if a child was engaged in something like biting it would only mean we would need to keep him away from other children and other people in general. Then there was the possibility of lawsuits, etc. Our entire world started to look as if it was going to change forever. Okay, I can handle the involuntary muscle spasms, head shaking and the vocal tics, and even the running, but biting?! Come on God, where in the heck are you? Houston, we have a problem! God, you cannot be watching what is going on here! Those were the thoughts that were in my head when I was away from the crowds, and away from the family.

The biting was something that neither we nor the doctors saw coming. When a child tries to bite their parents, better yet their grandmother, you can come to an accurate conclusion that it's probably not a game or a voluntary action.

Well, it didn't matter whether it was voluntary or not, it was very scary and needed to be addressed. On top of that, understandably, he wanted very badly to be treated like the other kids. How do you tell your child that you cannot allow them to be around other children because there is a fear that they may bite someone and that may result in big trouble for everyone? Thank God there were no reported occurrences at his school, but we were still without answers for why the running and biting was happening.

The only outlets we had were a few very close and trusted friends who did not mind taking on the risk of caring for Sherrod, no matter what was going on. He needed a place to hang out. If you don't have friends who will walk with you through challenging times, you may want to re-evaluate and re-invest into those who will be with you through the good, the bad and the very ugly storms of life. We all need friends like that. Hopefully you have a few people you are willing to stand in the gap for you as well.

Visiting his friends was also a chance for Ann and me to get some rest. Although we understood it could mean we were asking another family to possibly take on the weight of being up most of the night, it was a grand opportunity to re-charge. Unless you experience having most of your evenings interrupted by a crisis, it may be difficult for you to understand what it means to treasure a quiet one.

Many of these visits did result in telephone calls asking for our assistance with Sherrod. I vividly remember one occasion. It was a Friday evening and the end of a long work and school week. Shawn was busy with his band school friends attending a band competition. He played the trumpet. Sherrod was very excited to have a chance to blend into a different surrounding. He was preparing to go off to his buddy's house for a sleepover. We had our fingers crossed because we understood that this could turn into a very short or very long evening, either was not good. This was a big deal. We were probably more excited than he was just to be able to sleep for a night. He packed a bag with all of his video games and PlayStation, which was the game to have at that time. Off we were on our way to a friend's home 20 minutes away. After dropping him off, a few hours passed when Ann and I realized it was 10 p.m. and we had not heard from anyone. We thought no news is good news and started to believe it was going to be a good night.

I don't recall when we fell asleep but what I do remember is the knock at the door around 2 a.m. It was a very hard knock that woke me and Ann straight from our sleep. You would have thought it was the police! Well, as I started to gather myself and grab something to throw on, I could see through our curtains in the bedroom red and blue lights flashing and fading in and out. I rushed to the door only to meet up with, yes; you guessed it, the local police. He indicated that a friend of mine had been desperately trying to contact me about my son. He said "Sir, apparently your son isn't feeling well and after many attempts by phone, your friend contacted us." I politely thanked the officer for arriving and assured him that I would take care of the matter. I then went back into the house to alert Ann that Sherrod wasn't feeling well, and we needed to head out to see what was going on.

Ann and I honestly did not hear the three calls followed by voice messages letting us know that there was a problem. We were so tired that once our heads hit those pillows, it was as if we were in the deepest sleep ever. Back in those days cell phones were less popular but most people had an answering machine that recorded missed calls. We listened to the messages, and they sounded like this: First message: beep... "Hey West, (that's what friends usually called me) I don't think Sherrod is feeling well, pick up." Second message came approximately 15 minutes later: beep... "West, where are you!? You need to call me ASAP! Sherrod is having one of his episodes!" After that I can't recall how many other times he called, but the last recorded call sounded like this: "West! I can't believe that you are not picking up this phone!" He joked around a lot about our very long telephone cord.

I can only imagine him thinking: "you have enough cord on that phone to reach the entire house! Pick up the phone!" After listening to those messages, it was obvious he was serious, and it showed once the police arrived. When we reached our friends home to pick Sherrod up, he sat in their living room with his little overnight bag in his lap. He looked as if he had ruined everyone's night and was very sorry for it all. I felt bad about him not being able to complete an entire evening with his friend and that it was not his fault the night ended early. Hearing that family talk about what happened hours before sounded like a replay of events that we had witnessed night after night. They explained what they saw and the way his muscle spasms kicked in reminded them of a movie of someone being demon possessed. They explained, he levitated from his back into the air approximately three feet and back down while at the same time kicking their plant at least two times, all in one motion. They said it was incredible to see.

We thanked them for their hospitality, gave them hugs and loaded up to head back home. The ride home was very quiet with small comments to Sherrod. We tried to reassure him that he was not to blame for having T.S. and we understood how he felt being disappointed for not being able to stay at his friend's house. I often recall that night either with my friend and sometimes alone. Our family endured an array of emotions that night. We went from being excited for the things to come to having the authorities inform us of a problem. It reminds me of always remembering where my true help comes from. It's easy to lean and depend on people, places, and things that consistently give you the results you want, correct? For example, if I know that a particular restaurant serves the best food, my expectation is that they will not disappoint. In most cases, this would be correct. Every so often, you may take a chance and try another restaurant that serves similar food. Although there is no high expectation established with the new restaurant, there is an unstated expectation of what the food should taste like. If that expectation is not met, we go back to what meets our expectation. Sometimes I find that when I try new things outside of what I know works; I set myself up for possible disappointments. The Bible says in Psalms 22:5 that if we trust in God, we won't be disappointed. That would tell me that when I put my trust in anything else, I set myself up to be disappointed at some point. Although I know that with my head, my heart wants to believe I can trust others the way I trust God. Since God is jealous, our disappointment came from the trust we placed in our friends over the trust we should have placed in God. Looking back, Ann and I may have been a little too excited about looking forward to a good night's sleep. God reminded us that night that we were still in a fight and the only way we could win was if He fought for us.

## Outtake

Just when we believed things were going to get better, things got worse!  There is no way anyone could have prepared us for the various levels of challenges we were experiencing in this chapter.  It seemed as if things were piling up.  I was ready to accept Sherrod having T.S. and all the things the family needed to do for him to have a positive quality of life.  It was hard to try to accept the facts, but it was looking as if we needed to adapt to a new life.

The running and biting threw us for a loop! Bishop T.D. Jakes said "At every level there is another devil." I'm not sure where the quote originated but I heard it from him.  I would like to put a spin on that quote and say at every level there is a new opportunity to become stronger in your faith.  If someone would have communicated either quote to me when this chapter was being walked out, I'm not sure what my response would have been, but I'm pretty sure it would not have been nice. I truly believe the only reason we respond with anxiety and fear during tough times is because we really don't know how much we are capable of enduring. The Bible says that God knows what we can bear (1 Cor 10:13).

It's great for loved ones and friends to have a scripture ready when you are going through a tough time. I'm a preacher's kid (P.K.) and I know some scripture, but it's one thing to know scripture and another to live scripture. I wasn't living out scripture. So, although I may have heard true and encouraging words during that time, and I did, some of them landed in places of guilt, shame and conviction in my heart. I thought, why should God hear me when I'm not living a life that honors him?

Discovering the biting was something that I really didn't believe our family could handle. We could not sustain another blow! Our backs were already up against the wall and now with these new developments, all I could imagine was all the new challenges that were about to come our way. Questions started to flood my head; here are a few I recall:

- Will he be able to ever be in a social setting?
- Will he live with us forever?
- What about his education?
- Will he have friends who love him for who he is?

I'm sure there were more but I want you to understand that as I was filtering all these questions through my head, God was cleansing them in my heart. The only way to receive answers is to have a question. I'm so glad God heard my questions. The awesome thing about God is that He didn't judge me for having the questions. He filtered my questions through a plan that He had already purposed for my good. I believe that, just like with our earthly fathers, God does not mind entertaining questions. Actually He has already provided the answers to questions we have yet to ask! As you continue to read this story you will become aware of how God answered those questions. I've heard a saying that some things need to get worse before they can get better. The journey that God had our family on points to this statement being true for our situation. The worse in our eyes needed to happen so that the best could be revealed. The best is yet to come!

# Chapter 5

## Heart Check

The way things were progressing with the running, biting and muscle spasms continuing so frequently, we were faced with some difficult decisions. Honestly, all we wanted was help for our son. We really didn't want to place him in a facility of any kind because of the horror stories we heard, and we weren't sure if that was even the direction we should go. On the other hand, Sherrod's characteristics started to change. He began hallucinating. It really scared us into trying to respond quickly. Sometimes responding quickly leaves out other options that should have been weighed, but we were under pressure, and it caused us to react before we prayed.

I want to encourage any parent by saying that it's perfectly normal not to know what to do when faced with a life crisis that involves your child. The decisions we make should be grounded from love, not fear. I must admit, we were operating a little out of love but a lot out of fear. Since we didn't know if the hallucinations were coming from the medication or Sherrod's condition, we made the hard decision to take him in for a consultation at the Child Psychiatric Unit in Pennsylvania.

The initial meeting was just Ann and me talking about the journey we were on with Sherrod and his battle with what everyone was describing as T.S. As we spoke with the doctor, I could see there were other kids walking around the unit who were dealing with various disabilities. Some were dealing with anger issues and others with depression, and yet others with deeper challenges. We explained to the doctor that we had discovered something – the biting and the running - that not even the other doctors could understand about Sherrod's condition. After that initial talk we concluded that the hallucinations were probably coming from the strong medication. We also informed them that Sherrod was a very well-mannered child and was not a discipline problem but possibly needed some psychological help. I guess that statement wasn't foreign to them because they didn't hesitate to let us know that if a biting incident occurred at their facility, any child, including mine, would be placed in isolation and basically placed on punishment for their infraction. We assured them that the biting was totally involuntary, and this was the reason we were there.

Ann and I went back to the house to pray and talk through what we thought would be the right move. A few hours later the entire family gathered. We would have a talk with Sherrod and try to explain to him what was about to happen. It was one of the hardest conversations any parent could have with a child. As we sat at the kitchen table, I could see in his little eyes he was bracing himself. He looked so humble and hopeless, as if he was aware whatever we were about to share wasn't going to be good. I sat at my usual dinner spot which was at the head of the table nearest the garage while Ann sat to my left. Sherrod sat in his usual seat across from Ann and to my right and Shawn stood in the corner. As we began to explain our plans to visit the hospital, his eyes filled up with tears and they began to flow down his face. We basically explained to him that we were exploring every avenue possible to get him the best help we could and the place we were looking at was at the hospital. We also explained that this was an experiment, and it would only be for a few days. He repeatedly pleaded that we reconsider and give him another chance to be good. The entire house was in tears as we packed a few items for his overnight stay. Shawn stood quietly with his head down as if to indicate he was also struggling with our decision. I remember him and Sherrod exchanging a long hug and goodbye. That was a deep brother exchange.

It was yet early evening and the ride back to the hospital was very quiet. I don't believe there were two words shared as we drove the twenty minutes back to the facility. We entered the Psychiatric Unit and were met by the facilitator for the evening shift. People who work night shift have a different kind of temperament or vibe than day shift people. I'm not sure what it is, but it's just a thing. I've heard some say that God never meant for mankind to work through the night, only during the day. I don't know if that's an accurate statement, but I will say that when I worked the mid-day (some call it swing shift) and night shift (we called it the graveyard shift) I acted and functioned differently.

Ann and I stood in the hallway with his bags in our hands talking with this gentleman about the rules of engagement. He explained that there was a board, which he pointed towards on an adjacent hallway wall that listed all the kids who they labeled as *problems*. I thought that was interesting especially since the kids were there because they had various challenges. There were approximately ten names posted, which to this day I'm not sure of the significance. It may have been a way to embarrass them into conformance or something. Anyway, we stared at the board and quickly explained that Sherrod was not a discipline problem, and he probably would end up helping some of the kids. He was the kind of child that had a heart for those with disabilities. I'm sure it had something to do with how having one himself made him feel. As a matter of fact, to this very day he still has a heart for those with disabilities.

The energy coming from the facilitator as we stood in that hallway wasn't positive. Sherrod turned to us and said, "Mom and Dad, please don't leave me here. I don't like this place." We ignored him while trying to pay attention to the facilitator, but he continued louder. "I don't like it here, Mom and Dad, please take me home!" Then out of nowhere, he began trying to bite the facilitator! As I held him back, he started to cry and tell us that he just wanted to go home. He pleaded that he would do better and that he was sorry for his involuntary actions. To be transparent, from our initial conversations, I didn't really have a good feeling about this facilitator either. He treated every child we saw him interact with as if they were all discipline problems and if they should get out of line, they would end up on the board of shame where all could see. Ann being an educator and me coming from a military environment agreed this method was a little too abrasive based on the outcomes they desired. But hey, they were the experts and we needed help, so we went with it. We had come to get help and as hard as it was to leave Sherrod there, we decided to do so. As he continued to cry, we turned to him, gave him a hug, told him we loved him, and then turned him over to the facilitator.

As we walked away, he shouted, "Mom and Dad, please don't leave me here, please, please don't leave me here!" We continued to walk away with tears in our eyes as his voice echoed off the hospital walls. It was quiet in the hospital at that time, and we could hear his cries all the way to the exit doors. The ride home was as quiet as if we were sitting in a library. I was trying to hold it together driving while my tears blocked my vision. I could hear Ann sobbing quietly with her head facing her window, trying not to let me see the pain on her face. We didn't say much at all, but we reassured each other that we had done the best for both him and us. Even as I recall this moment in writing, it brings with it some deep emotion.

Moments after arriving to the house there was a message on the answering machine letting us know that we needed to return to the hospital to bring our son more clothing for a four-day stay. The goal was to have the doctors observe him for a few days and conclude as to why he was experiencing some of the things we saw, such as biting and running. The confusing part was trying to relate it to someone with T.S. We gathered additional clothes and made the trip back to the hospital. It was approximately 9 p.m. when we arrived back at the facility. At this time, the hospital was rather empty since visiting hours had ended.

It was scary walking down a very dim corridor not seeing doctors or nurses. It was gloomy as if we were in a scary movie or something. I was holding Ann's hand trying to comfort her, but she was also comforting me. We walked down the quiet halls only hearing the echo of our own footsteps. When we arrived at the check-in area, we identified ourselves and asked the young lady behind the desk if she knew the whereabouts of our son. She paged the night facilitator who met us at the desk. He explained that there had been an incident where Sherrod had tried to bite him and since there was a no-tolerance rule for things like that, he had been placed in isolation. We explained once again with frustration that the biting was involuntary and that our son was not a discipline problem! I could see Ann was upset and so was I. We demanded to see him. He walked us to an area that resembled a row of enclosed racquetball courts. It reminded me of a jail for kids without bars or windows. We could hear Sherrod from a distance crying and pleading to be released.

When the door was opened where he was located, he ran to Ann explaining that he didn't mean to try and bite the facilitator and that they were being very mean to him. He stated that they placed him in a head lock and were rough with him. We told him that we understood but he needed to try very hard to obey what the facilitator was asking of him. He continued to plead for us to take him with us, but we had made our decision and wanted to stick with it. It was a very sad moment for sure. We turned and walked away to the cries and pleads he shouted, "Please, Mom and Dad! I'm sorry! I will try and do better, please don't leave me here!" As we exited the hollow racquetball type room, he continued to cry. It seemed as though his voice was ringing throughout the entire hospital. As much as we knew we were doing the right thing, the pain of seeing and hearing your child cry out for your help and you not reciprocate, must be one of the worst feelings a parent can experience. That's where we were.

As we left the facility for the third time, we ran into a friend who was a member of our church and just so happened to be a doctor intern on staff at the hospital. We told her a short summary of our story. She vowed to make sure she would check on our little guy every day to ensure he was receiving the best care. We were so grateful to have someone on staff making sure he was okay while we were away. It made for a comfort level that helped us relax a bit more, considering we did not have any control over what could happen while we were away from him. We never really told her how important that exchange in the parking lot of that hospital meant. It was not just a coincidence she arrived when she did. That moment meant everything to us. God sent an angel in disguise. It was as if He was saying, "By the way, let me send you something or someone to remind you I'm with you. When you think you are totally helpless, God will reassure you that He has your best interest at hand. Even when the enemy tries to go above and beyond the afflictions that God permits, He will place a hedge of protection around you so that the devil is reminded of his limitations. God sent this doctor to our rescue at the right time to make sure that if there was any foul play going on that an angel had been dispatched as cover and protection. Oh, that's so good! This doctor marched over to that facility and introduced herself to the administration and let them know that she was a friend of the family and would be checking in to see how things were going. How do you like that? God had placed a hedge of protection around our son. I'm not saying there was anything foul going on or even that the devil was in it, but just in case, God provided a safety net.

He would stay at the facility for three days. After the first night, we returned back to speak with the doctors. First, they informed us that after we left the night prior, Sherrod was released from isolation and went to his room and fell asleep without assistance. This was quite a surprise and a miracle for us to hear. We struggled trying to help him with going to sleep every night for a very long time. Soon, Sherrod would join the meeting. Although the traits of his T.S. were evident with the twitching of his body and the stomping of his feet, he seemed to be in good spirits. The doctor explained that they were not sure they could conclude why Sherrod was portraying additional traits that were not consistent with someone with T.S. - specifically the running and biting - but they would keep an eye out for the next few days. Sherrod expressed good feelings about the other kids in the facility and told us that he wanted to stay there.

We left with at least a positive assurance about him adjusting to his new environment. On day two, Ann and I arrived to find that our son had taken on a leadership role and many of the other children in the unit were following his leadership. This was not a real surprise to us because we knew he had a heart for those with disabilities. He went from being placed on the disciplinary board to being the leader of the unit in two days! Almost like going from the pit to the palace. Do you remember the story about Joseph in the Bible? Sherrod had become a little Joseph in that facility. He had been placed in solitary confinement and reassigned to a leadership role in the palace.

Alright, it wasn't a palace, but I hope you understand the analogy.

When we arrived on day three the doctors didn't have any answers to our questions or the problems that lead us to admit him. Their observations only encouraged us and pointed us to try other medications that might help him function at a higher level, but there were no answers for the running and biting. Ann and I did notice that whenever Sherrod was experiencing anxiety, whether it was while doing homework or what he felt was a negative energy, it would trigger running and biting. Somewhere along the way, thank God that part faded away either from the change in meds or a change in him. But the vocal tics, shaking of his body, stomping, and blinking of the eyes were still evident.

The one thing that was very encouraging as a result of going to the hospital was Sherrod left that facility full of courage and hope. His encouragement was not so much for himself but more for the kids around him with issues he felt were greater than his own.

Many times, if we take the focus off of our own situations and focus on someone else's, it will place us in a totally different mind-set. It helps us become more considerate, patient, humble and a host of other adjectives that are by-products of a grateful heart. It's very easy to believe that our situation is the gravest until we discover that someone else's is greater. I believe you would quickly thank God for not having to deal with whatever you saw as a greater challenge.

I remember when we were saying our goodbyes to staff and patients. There were many tears and hugs. Sherrod left there with the names of many of the kids and was trying to schedule when he could plan a return visit, just to let the other kids know he was thinking about them.

You see, God will give you peace while you are in your valley. This was a day of peace, and we were so grateful to receive a little of it while still trying to find our way out of our valley.

**Outtake**

I wish I could articulate the raw feelings I was experiencing when we decided to visit the psychiatric unit of the hospital. The memory of those moments is still etched in my mind. There were feelings of failure on my part for not having a better solution for our child. Sherrod was feeling as though he was the problem. This is why he continued to promise to do better. Hearing him utter those words time and time again only made me hurt more. Although we kept reminding him that he was not responsible for having T.S., he continued to place the blame on himself. I also felt as though God had let us down for not showing up in a different way. Yes, I wanted God to show up my way and in my time, but He didn't.

Each time I revisit this chapter to add comments or edits, I experience an emotional pull on my heart. We all felt some deep pain as the events began to unfold leading up to our decision. Leaving

Sherrod in an environment foreign to us was very scary. The amazing thing here is that God had us moving in a direction that we were not familiar with at all. As a matter of fact, the decision to place him in a facility for observation came directly after we consulted only with God. We did not consult friends, only God. It is important to also know that at that time there were a number of doctor interns attending our church. I'm not sure why we didn't seek guidance from any of them, but we didn't. To reassure us that God was in control and that we didn't need to fear, God sent an angel in the form of our friend who happened to be a doctor on staff. When you read about the encounter we had with her in that parking lot that night know that it was nothing short of a miracle. Please understand why this moment was so defining for us. It was life changing! We were pretty messed up leaving him there that dreadful night. Honestly, it felt to me as though we had given up and all we could do was hand him over to someone else.

The fact that she showed up in the middle of the pain we were experiencing lets me know just how much God cares about each and every one of us.

He doesn't allow pain in our lives to reside just because He can. He allows it on purpose for a purpose. When that purpose is completed, He sends His rescue team! Just as he had done in the past, God rescued us once again. I hope you are seeing what continues to happen with this story. Each and every time our backs are against the wall and we can't see our way out, God shows up! I'm telling you it's not magic and it's not by chance. The Bible says in Colossians 1:13-14 (MSG) that God rescued us from dead-end alleys and dark dungeons. At that time we were definitely at a dead-end and it was pretty dark for sure.

Here is a word of encouragement for you, my friend. Please remember that when you are in the middle of some of life's challenges and you are trying to see your way out, whatever you decide to do, God is with you. Even if you make a mistake, He is with you. I'm not sure our decision to admit our son into the hospital was a mistake or ordained by God. We did consult Him but I would be misleading you if I said God told us to do what we did. I'm not sure if that even matters. Remember, He is a rescuer. So in order to be rescued, someone needs to be in trouble. I'm not trying to insinuate that making mistakes doesn't often bring negative consequences, but when you have God in your corner, mistakes can turn into miracles. You may be in trouble and you may believe the mess you are in needs intervention. Trust me; the rescuer of your soul is also the rescuer of your situation. He is never too late and he is definitely right on time. As you think about your own situation, I want you to remember what happened to us when we were in a very dark place. Think about the timing of God and how He knew exactly when it was time to rescue us. He also knows exactly when to rescue you as well. It may feel as though you are abandoned, but you are not.

There is purpose behind why your rescuer has not arrived "yet". I'm praying you grabbed the last word in the previous sentence. *Yet* means it's in your best interest to continue to wait. It means that God has a plan even when you make mistakes. I'm a witness. Wait, I say, on the Lord, He is on the way.

# Chapter 6

## Next Stop

Here we were on this journey, not knowing where it would take us. Our family had relocated to be closer to work, church and the friends with whom we spent most of our time. We also transitioned from one middle school to another. Sherrod was blessed to have the best care he could possibly receive going into a new middle school. Although he had awesome teachers who genuinely cared for him, he also had his Mom in the same building teaching other students. She was there if he needed her, and there were days when he did. After one year, he would move on to become a freshman in high school and 15 years old. He was in yet another new environment in a different school and away from Mom. We sensed we were in for a long ride.

Have you ever ridden on a commuter train? I recently retired from a position that required I commute to and from work on a train. I did this for more than a decade. It was a ride full of all sorts of activities. As a matter of fact, this book could have been completed long before its publication from the time I've spent on the train, but there were too many distractions. Since my commute was approximately two hours one-way, I had the pleasure of hearing the conductors make various announcements as we made our journey down the tracks. As we approached each stop, the conductor would announce where we were and which doors along the very long train ride would open to allow passengers to exit and board. Each time we arrived at the end of the line (trip) they would utter, "ladies and gentlemen, the final stop will be Philadelphia. All doors will open, please watch your step; there is a gap between the train and the platform. Thank you for riding Amtrak, we hope you have a great day!" There were times they would let me announce a stop. It was usually my own. I'm thinking that was so I would stop talking about how much better I could make the announcements.

Often times when we are struggling with an issue that seems insurmountable like ours seemed, some decide they might as well give up. Let's tell the truth. Many times, we say that, and we haven't even done all we can, and we still decide to de-board before we should. It might not be your stop on the journey, but you decide that since you have been traveling for some time and seen so many sights (opinions) you might as well just get off at the next stop. The only problem with that decision is once you do that, you must decide what you are going to do once you de-board.

On our journey with Sherrod during this time, so many people gave their opinions. Some said don't give up trying to find answers while others said accept your situation and move on with your life. There are plenty of resources you can get to help you cope. Ann and I didn't believe in our hearts that we should give up trying to find answers for Sherrod, and Sherrod didn't want to give up either. But the journey was making us weary, and we all wanted to rest. In an effort not to appear depleted or defeated we would say the "right" things around the "right" people. We knew how to put on the plastic smile and act as though we were handling the situation just right. But the truth is, we were scared as heck and just wanted to get off at the next stop.

We began listening to what the doctors were saying about Sherrod's condition and started losing the grip of faith we once held. They reassured us that there were other children and families who were living with T.S. We collected pamphlets of programs and information about conferences that were being held in the area that we could attend. This would help us gain tools that would help us settle into an adjusted lifestyle. You see, settling is just another way of saying, "this is good enough." If you settle, you are saying you are getting off at the next stop. Although we were tired and just wanted to rest, the Spirit of God inside of us whispered, "don't get off at the next stop."

In the meantime, Sherrod believed he could do whatever he wanted to do even though his condition was worsening as he got older. The high school he attended extended his learning support classes his first year there even though he was an independent and bright kid with good grades. He only needed learning support primarily for extended test taking time and math.

We also knew that at times when he felt pressured, his T.S. would flare up. During test times, he would take breaks so that he would not get overwhelmed. Early on we would receive calls from the school about him having challenges with focusing in class. There were other times we would need to pick him up because he was experiencing headaches or just not feeling well. He learned how to cope in this new environment where peers can be less accepting and friendly, but he was determined to fit in.

One of these moments occurred when he decided he wanted to try out for the freshmen basketball team. Remember, this is a kid with T.S., but he wanted so badly to make the team. We prayed that he would succeed because he was not making many friends at his new school. I can recall my early high school days trying to "fit in" by trying out for the basketball and football teams. The coaches let the guys know early on which days they would determine first, second and final cuts. At each phase throughout the process, they would post on the bulletin board which players were moving on to the next level. If you didn't see your name, it only meant you were being let go or what we called "cut." That was an agonizing feeling hoping to find your name on that board. In those days, making the team was like a badge of honor. To my dismay, on one account, mine wasn't there so I decided I would not try out for any other high school sports to avoid the pain of not feeling good enough. I would later become a pretty good all-around sports guy in the neighborhood. I became competitive. I would match up with some of the guys who made the team during pickup games, and many times come out on top.

We were trying to shield Sherrod from the pain of rejection as best we could. He had already experienced some of that in the classroom so we hoped he would somehow, someway, be selected. Now I will say, he was a pretty good basketball, soccer and football player coming up and as I recalled earlier, he always had tremendous speed. Although we had not previously had conversations about trying out for any of the high school sports teams, somehow Sherrod knew something about acceptance and sports. He knew one way to be accepted, especially in a new school, is to become a member of a team sport. I have no idea how he figured that out, but he did. It may have been from the pee-wee games we attended with him while I was in the military. He really tried hard to succeed. He would come home from some of those practices and give us a blow-by-blow and most of it was about some of the other students laughing at and/or others even bullying him. If you know anything about Sherrod, whether you have time or not, he is going to tell you the WHOLE story from top to bottom. It usually ends hours later.

One day he came home and explained that he didn't make the final cut. I remember that day because it took me back in time. The same pain I felt when I didn't see my name on that bulletin board surfaced again. As I searched for words to come out of my mouth, he pulled out a basketball jersey from his book bag smiling from ear to ear and said "Sike, (indicating he was joking) I made the team, Mom and Dad!" Ann and I almost said "WHAT", in harmony as to indicate, you have got to be kidding. It shows you where our faith really was, huh? That was a great day. We could not believe what he had accomplished. This was huge! He explained that the coach said that he had worked so hard, and that he was such a great encourager. He would lead the team in prayer before practices and games. This was such a bright spot for him because it made him feel as though he had conquered something.

The Bible speaks about training your children up so that when they become older, they will remember the things they were taught and not cast those things aside (Prov 22:6). When the boys were in grade school, Ann and I (mostly Ann) used to have them recite Philippians 4:13 almost every morning before going to school. Even now, as adults, every so often we remind them of that scripture when they come to us with some of the challenges they face in life. The remarkable thing about scripture is when it's applied and it comes alive for you in your situation(s), it gives you fuel for the next hurdle. It reminds you that God doesn't lie and that if you have faith and believe, you can do whatever you set your heart to do if it aligns with His plans for your life.

Sherrod believed he could make that basketball team! He would go on to play the entire season. He wasn't as much a vital part on the court as he was off the court. There are times when we purpose to do things for one reason and God purposes it for another. The Bible talks about this in Prov 19:21. So, it was Sherrod's purpose to make the team and God said, "I'm going to make that happen for another reason, Sherrod. I want you to represent me in that locker room." He would lead those guys in prayer before every game and was given the title of Team Chaplain. He was proud of that position and wore it well. We would go to his games and watch him. Although he didn't get much playing time, he was like a little coach on the bench. As the guys would come out of the game from doing the best they could, he would pat them on their backs or shake their hand to indicate a job well done. He was walking out a purpose that God had planned.

The road to our expected end is not always the one we imagine, being clear of traffic jams, potholes, and detours. Many of these obstacles in our way are the things designed to help develop us into the men and women God has always intended us to be. I heard someone once say that the boulder that you are trying to push out of your way is not intended to be moved. Instead, its use is to develop the muscles you are using in the process. God is building spiritual muscles in us through the challenges we encounter in life. In 1 Peter 5:10 it says that trials come to make us strong. I know Ann and I didn't feel very strong as we went through this process but because we believed what our eyes could not see and trusted in the God that said He would never leave us or let us down, we held on for dear life. There is also a scripture in the Bible in 2 Corinthians 12 where Paul is speaking about his weaknesses. He came to the realization that God is magnified when we come to a place in life that we become helpless. He shows up big when we acknowledge we have come to the end of ourselves and what we thought we could handle. We realize we can't succeed without His help. There is a reason for testimonies. They are meant to encourage others to stay in the fight! They are a part of God's glorious resume and a reminder to those who may get weary that there is an expected end to your journey. Listen for the conductor's call. He is about to let you know that you have arrived at your appointed destination, but before He calls your stop, He has some things He wants you to experience along the way.

Take a look at your surroundings, and the people, places, and things you see. Most importantly, keep your eyes fixed on where you are headed. There are faith buddies around you that will help you stay focused. Embrace the ride. Next stop is your expected end - watch your step.

## Outtake

I think I have a better understanding of the reason why some fathers try to direct some of the accomplishments or missteps of their kids. Some try to extend a legacy they helped build and others try to save loved ones from the pain of failure they once experienced. When Sherrod announced his desire to try out for the high school basketball team, I became one of those dads that wanted to shield him from the pain of failure. He was already dealing with a disability and we did not need something traumatic to cause further setbacks. I didn't feel the need to push the envelope; things were better than they had been in a while. On one account I wanted him to fit in with the other kids and on the other hand, I was trying to shield him from the very things that kids do. Again, as I stated in this chapter, I'm not sure how Sherrod came to the conclusion that making the basketball team would be a game changer, but he was right and it was indeed.

As I think back on the motivation I had to shield Sherrod from failure, I have to admit, the reason I was trying to shield him was because of my own fear of not trying again. I used the example earlier about fathers trying to influence their kids' accomplishments or missteps, but it applies to mothers and daughters as well. Sometimes, parents, our negative experiences pertaining to a similar life event can cripple the possibility of a different outcome if we intervene. If Sherrod would have come home and told us that he didn't make the basketball team, I probably would have tried very hard to persuade him not to pursue that road again. Sherrod's outcome may have turned out different if he would have tried to make the team again, but because of my fear, I would have blocked the possibility of a different outcome.

I'm so glad he made the team the first time around because it saved me from being a possibility blocker.

I believe the experiences we have in life should be shared. They should be shared from a place of learning and growing. Our children are made from us, but our children are not us. They have their own wants and desires. We are to guide them, not dictate what they should or should not do. I know it's hard! Believe me, parenting from a distance is hard stuff, but it's necessary if growth is to take place at the right pace. Remember, Sherrod wanted to make the team so that he would be accepted by his peers and God purposed him to make the team for a bigger reason. God knew that those kids on the team may have had better basketball skills than he did, but what He also knew was that what they were lacking is what Sherrod had. He gave them encouragement through Sherrod. He gave them support through Sherrod. He gave them affirmation through Sherrod and He gave them acknowledgement through Sherrod. I'm trying to convey here that it's important for us as parents to guide our children in the ways of the Lord. It's important that they understand that we made mistakes when we were their age and we still make them today. We have to also honor and respect them for who they are and what they do. Some of their ways are not like ours. Some of their thoughts are not like ours either. If we have or are training them the right way; our trust should be in God, not our past experiences. He has a plan for them just like He has for us. Letting go is hard. Not letting go also makes life harder for the one we are holding.

Just as Sherrod walked down a path similar to mine, the results he received were different. This lesson helped me understand a lot about what God placed in him that helped him believe he could achieve what he did. Actually, God places this kind of fight in all of us.

Whether you have achieved a lot at something or failed at something else, what happened with you may not happen with your child. Guess what? The results they receive may prove to help them become who God intended them to be, not so much what you or I currently see.

# Chapter 7

## The Call

Moving through the first year in high school, during and after basketball, presented its ups and downs for the family. Sherrod was still on the prescribed medication from his doctor, and we were also allowing him to stay home on days he could not get going. His T.S. would flare up to the point that it prevented him from being around others. Just so you can have a clear picture of what I'm trying to convey, this meant that his body was extremely out of control with some of the symptoms we discussed earlier. During those times, he could not function in a classroom setting without there being a visual distraction to the entire class and embarrassment for himself.

We honestly didn't have a clue where to turn, but I want to stress, there was something going on with the family that kept us smiling behind the tears and praising God for what we were yet to see. That is all a part of this faith walk. Faith isn't faith if you know the way in which God is going to work things out. Faith believes in the expected outcome before it arrives. I heard someone say that faith is not knowing how God will deliver the outcome but letting Him know that you trust His character. We had our eyes on God. We trusted what we believed the outcome would be, but we had no idea when, where or how it would happen. One thing we were sure about is that we didn't want to skip a day or two of medication! That would result in a night filled with some of what we covered in previous chapters with the family ending up in the nearest emergency room. We were adamant about Sherrod taking his medicine on time every day. Like with other medicines previously prescribed to him, the one he was on started out great and slowly but surely became less effective. We were being encouraged with some victories and discouraged with what we determined as losses. Yet we were always holding on.

As the year progressed, we were praying and watching as our little guy, who was not so little anymore, worked his way through his freshmen year. He was determined to fit in. It was as if he was ignoring the fact that he had any issues in his life and wanted to just be seen as "normal." Sometimes being what the world calls normal is abnormal, but that's another conversation and possibly another book. But the challenge with being a teen is that the cliques and social groups that are very hard to become a part of if you aren't known as a childhood friend or a super popular kid. Sherrod didn't have either under his belt, so he was the odd man out, especially with a disorder added to that. Again, he didn't quit doing whatever he needed to do <u>to not be</u> noticed. That's right; he didn't want to be noticed as the kid with a problem. He didn't want to be noticed as the kid walking into a special needs classroom. He didn't want to be noticed as the kid who left school periodically because he had an episode in class. He just didn't want to be noticed.

One thing I do know is for something to be noticed, it must be seen. God was using Sherrod's T.S. so that His miracle could be seen. He calls us out of darkness into the light. Light exposes. Unfortunately, you can't stand in the light and not be seen. The reason for exposure is for you and others to see something that may not have been noticeable if there was no light. Sherrod didn't like being seen having T.S. It's sad to see anyone experience not having control of their faculties. 1 Pet 2:9 says, we are chosen to proclaim the excellences of him who called us out of darkness into the light. It's a calling! God is calling every one of us out of something into something else. He was calling Sherrod out of T.S. into healing, His way.

The entire family was walking it out. God often works on several scenarios at the same time when it comes to healing, deliverance, blessings, challenges, etc. He is the great multi-tasker! Don't tell me multi-tasking doesn't work. Ask God! That's why He is God. He can work on a world crisis and at the same time make sure He fixes your situation at home. He can bring peace among two world nations, and at the same time answer your prayer to bring your son or daughter home from a war. He is the great I AM! Thinking back, all we really needed to do was walk things out. I know now that the situation our family had to face with this health challenge was about a calling from God. He wants His name glorified and sometimes He chooses people like you and I to walk out the process that will ultimately bring Him that glory.

This calling was from God to the West Family. People were watching and we were doing our best to act and seem as if everything was fine in our household. In John chapter 6, Jesus asked Peter if he and the rest of the disciples would walk away from him as thousands of others had done that day. Peter replied, "where would we go?" He believed Jesus was his refuge and the only one who could protect him. Peter and the rest of the twelve disciples had history with Jesus, and if God was to be for them, who could be against them?

So, with our situation we also had history with God, and we knew that if God wasn't going to rescue us from this situation, no one could. I stated in the beginning of this chapter that faith is not knowing how God will show up but letting him know that you believe He will. You can think that something is going to work out, but the faith part is trusting God is going to show up. I know it can sometimes feel hopeless when we are going through challenges in life, but believe this, God's got a story He is writing with your life and if you let Him complete His story, it's going to be an ending with a twist that nobody expected, but Him.  After all, where are you going to go if you leave Him?   I'm sure you do not have a better option, but many try another way and many fail to see Him working it out for their good.  They fail to go through the process.  Sad to say, I have witnessed so many who have walked away from the grace and cover of God because they felt abandoned by Him. The problem is, it's a feeling not a reality and just as feelings are, they come and go.  God doesn't come and go.  He is the only true and consistent factor in our lives.  If I were with Peter during that time, I would have probably given him a high five when he made that statement and repeated it out loud, "yeah Jesus, where are we going to go?" with sarcasm.

God had laid such a firm foundation with us through many that came before us.  He is the game changer!  All we knew was to at least try to trust Him.

Although as I stated, we had history with God as well, it amazes and saddens me, how many of us (I'm included) after challenges come, forget what God did in the past, and we start panicking. We get wrapped around our feelings and react to them instead of what we know or what we have known. Since I'm a worshipper you will read of me referencing songs that come to mind like "Do it Again" by Elevation Worship. This song speaks directly to the sovereignty of God and the history we have concerning His promises. All we have is His promises and the Bible says, He can't lie (Num 23:19). That same scripture talks about how God doesn't have to repent or say something that He doesn't carry out. God is bound to what He says, even if He would like to take it back. The contrast is man. Everything God can't do, we do. We lie, we say things that are not true, we don't keep our word and we must repent time and time again. He is the only being that is forever consistent. This is the reason He can require we hold fast to the things He has said and the things He has already done. He also helps us out with our faith walk by encouraging others who have experienced His miracle working power to testify about it, so that we are reminded of these things. These are the great cloud of witnesses that the Bible speaks about in Heb 12. God is asking us to trust His character when we can't understand His ways. Because of these factors, we were trying to hold on to what we believed despite not seeing the changes we desired. We started to focus too much on what we were seeing and not trusting totally on what God said. Were we afraid? Yes, we were! Were we confused? Yes, we were! Were we looking at our current situation and thinking we didn't know what was going to happen? Yes, we were! Were we thinking at times that perhaps this was just our plight? Yes, indeed! And with all that, we also had *shaken faith*. Our faith was unstable. We were having good days and bad and although we weren't always trusting God like we should, I believe God honored when we did. God requires we give Him something to work with. The Bible says in Matt 17:20 all we need is faith the size of a mustard seed. If we would just give God a little something He can work with. He will take your little bit and make it much to the world when it's all said and done. Your little bit becomes much when it's placed in God's hand. You are reading one account of that on these pages as God takes that little bit and blows our family's mind for His glory so that we could tell His story.

## Outtake

There is an old hymn we used to sing in our church when I was younger; it's called: Count Your Blessings. Some of the lyrics read: "Count your blessings; name them one by one. Count your blessings; see what God hath done." This song has a message laced through it that reminds the singer that God is always blessing us, one way or another. Counting your blessings helps you be thankful for each one and changes the focus from what blessings you don't have and shifts the focus to what you do have. This is a hard reminder. We were experiencing some highs with Sherrod making the basketball team and the challenge was not losing focus on all the blessings God had given us leading up to this point. I think I'm a glass ½ full kind of person. In other words, I try to see the bright side of most situations. Even so, as positive as I try to be, I began to forget about all God had done and got lost in what had yet to be done. God had handed us so many wins along the way. The fact that from time to time we would lose hope about the future is pretty sad to even admit. Unfortunately, that is where we were. I'm not proud of our track record along this process, but I'm sure proud of God's. Although our faith and reliance on God was pretty shaky at times; He was always consistent and showed us His grace and favor along the way.

Making the basketball team was huge and we did celebrate that accomplishment, but it didn't solve all our problems. There were still some social obstacles yet to be faced and Sherrod was still experiencing some of the tics we described in some of the earlier chapters. Friends were still hard to come by but He did have some of his buddies from church who were very instrumental in helping him feel secure in some of the social settings at school. As you have probably noticed, sometimes we were up and sometimes we were down. Our goal is to get you to understand that we were experiencing the same feelings most people feel. We didn't want to paint a false narrative of a perfect family trusting God with all their hearts every step of the way. That would be a lie. What's very important to know about our story is that God used it all! He used our smiles and our frowns. He used our happiness and our sorrows. He used our celebrations and our closed door pity parties all to bring out what He purposed this journey to be. I wish I could tell you that the story God is writing in your life will end like you want it. That would make the plight of your journey pretty easy to predict. This would also mean we could know the mind of God and how He would handle each situation. The Bible tells us that no one can know His mind, so trying to understand His ways is beyond our capabilities. The reason your story can't match mine, as similar as they may be, is because we each are travelling towards our designed end in various seasons. I'm referencing different seasons from a standpoint of where we are with regard to our relationship with God. He moves on our behalf based on the gaps in that relationship. He uses each event we live out in order to bring us closer to Him and lessen the gap. Do not become overwhelmed with discouragement based on some type of setback or misstep you are currently experiencing. God will collect it all as He shapes and re-shapes what He is doing to mold you into what He wants you to be. Remember to celebrate and remember each victory along the way, whether they are large or small. It will help you remain thankful when your faith gets shaken. I mentioned in this chapter how Sherrod was doing all he could to be "normal" around his friends. God had another plan. He wanted Sherrod's condition on center stage with a spotlight. If a miracle is seen, there is no denying it happened. God was setting up something that could only be measured by the test of time. He was using Sherrod to make that happen. There is another song that comes to mind as I end this outtake. It's a song I used to hear the elderly sing in church. The name of the song is *"Hold on Just a Little While Longer"* written and performed by Rev. Cleophus Robinson Jr.

That song lets you know that everything is going to be alright. I'm here to tell you just that! Embrace the good, the bad and the ugly, it all matters. As much as we tried to hide the ugly parts of our journey, the more God purposed to use them. The parts of our lives that we would rather not mention or reveal are the very ones God wants to use the most.

# Chapter 8

## Is This My Hand?

The year would progress through Sherrod's freshman well into his sophomore year. Although we weren't experiencing major setbacks, we weren't experiencing major breakthroughs either. We were sort of just living our lives out with the cards that we were dealt. We were trying to be good parents and model what we thought was the right stuff. That means we were just trying to keep things quiet at school and at home. Sherrod, on the other hand, was pushing the envelope. What does that mean? He aspired to go to college! Remember, he was in a learning support class, and although we thought our son had remarkable perseverance, will, and smarts, we were also accepting the hand we had been dealt without complaints.

I can recall the meetings we had with some of his teachers and how they expressed their opinions about students in that program and the likelihood of them finishing high school, not to mention entering institutions of higher education. At that time, the statistics showed that no students had ever left that particular program and entered college. To be totally transparent, Ann and I weren't even concentrating on college for Sherrod; we were focused on healing. College was the last thing on our mind. But he wanted us to talk with the teachers about the possibility. Yes, at that point it was just a dream. Looking back at what we knew and what we had experienced, we thought no way! With Ann being a teacher and having our oldest son Shawn in college, we knew what the college entry process was all about. Sherrod had visited his brother's college campus a few times, and I believe eating and sleeping on a college campus might have sparked his vision for a college future. Nonetheless, college was on the shelf as far as Ann and I were concerned. He had made the basketball team. Isn't that enough? His life was an open book being played out before our eyes.

We knew who was calling the plays, but we were like Monday morning quarterbacks. We would have called a different play or declared a loss before the clock ran out.

I recall hearing a sermon while attending a conference by the renowned Dr., Deforest B. Soaries, *"How to Win with A Bad Hand."* He brilliantly articulated an analogy of someone with a deck of cards. Sometimes you may look at the cards of life that you have been dealt and think, this is a bad hand. If you aren't careful, you will believe that there is nothing you can do but fold, like Ann and I were starting to do. The Bible says that after you have done all just STAND! (Eph 6:13). Yes, there are some hands that may be bad in your eyes but just like with a card game, there is a game to be played. The game of life must be walked out and if you throw in the towel just because it looks bad, you may lose the game that you were destined to win.

There are times when God wants to use our situations to show others that we are more than conquerors when we are called to a thing. You see, being called means everything. If you are called to a thing, this means God has already supplied you with everything you need to succeed. This is why we should be careful about wanting what others have or wanting to be in someone else's shoes. God has a plan for your life that is custom-made just for you for a reason. We are all fearfully and wonderfully made. There are no replicas or carbon copies in His portfolio. If what you are going through in life has you shaken or hopeless, you must ask yourself a question: Are these the cards God dealt me, or are these someone else's? If it was destined by God, guess what? It's a fixed game. You win!

I'm not sure Ann and I believed we were dealt a bad hand, but we did believe we were in a fight. We didn't want to let God down, and we also wanted to show our boys that everything we were living was real.

At some point in this walk it becomes time to put up or shut up! It comes down to this, either we believe what the scriptures say and what we talk about, or we become bad witnesses of the gospel. We wanted to be good witnesses.

We were in Sherrod's 2nd year of high school, and the thoughts of going to college were a little late. The clock was running out. He had taken no college prep courses because we weren't focusing on college at all.

In the game of life, this seemed as if our team was about to take a loss. You know how it is when you are sitting at a sporting event, and you have been cheering your team on all game long, and your cheering is being drowned out by the scoreboard and the clock that is telling you time is running out? You start to pack up your stuff as you see others doing the same because of the obvious perceived outcome. People are exiting all around the stadium. Why? Because the clock is telling everyone that based on the score and the time left, it's inevitable that the outcome isn't going to be in favor of the losing team, which happens to be yours. So, you pack up your belongings and head for your vehicle. As you make your way, you hear a roar from the crowd. Something happened but you don't know what it is because you left the stadium. You may be thinking, "What just happened? What did I miss? Did that other team score again?" You and a host of others may have missed a spectacular play that changed the outcome of the game. I have been in that situation on a few occasions where I missed a play that changed everything in a game because I thought the game was over. In our situation, the clock was indeed ticking, and the outcome wasn't looking good. But there were still ticks left on the clock, and Sherrod must have thought, "this isn't over yet!" This is a reminder to us all. When God is in it, your situation is not over. He always has a timeout that he can choose to use at any moment. This means God can put a pause on whatever is going on by calling a spiritual timeout in your life that allows Him to re-evaluate your situation and adjust according to His will. The key is to never ever give up. Not all of the outcomes will be what you would like, but for sure, they will come out the way they should for your good. It's hard to see or understand that when we are in the middle of a battle, but rest assured the battle is not yours; it's the Lord's. In our situation, it reminds us that if there is time, we have time. Believing becomes the foundation from where you draw strength. It is also important to understand that believing becomes the prerequisite to receiving. Sherrod was one of the kids that just believed.

So here we were with yet another challenge staring us in the face. We have a child struggling to be accepted in an environment that is not real sensitive to people with disabilities. Here is a child that is in a learning support program with T.S. This same child throws what we call in football a "bomb." That's to indicate it is a long shot or attempt at reaching the desired destination. This is where the quarterback throws the football quite a distance to advance the ball down the field. This would be Sherrod's bomb. He wanted his parents and teachers to talk about how he could enter college. In the game of life, in my mind, this play should not have been called. We were celebrating the small victories we had won. After all, he was learning how to cope, and most students and teachers in his environment had begun to understand and accept his challenges.

Ann and I were starting to become somewhat comfortable with how things were shaping out, but

Sherrod was not comfortable with how he was shaping out. So, he threw a bomb as an attempt to advance his life further than we had ever planned and turned in the cards he believed weren't his to hold.

## Outtake

When Sherrod initially informed us that he wanted to attend college, I really didn't take it seriously. I actually thought he was being influenced by the visits he made to his brother's college and also by his friends who were planning trips to visit various colleges. Remember, he wanted to blend in and not be seen as odd or different. Our goal was to ensure he finished high school. I remember that feeling as a young teen. Many of my friends had colleges picked out by the time they were juniors and I didn't have a plan at all. I remember making up false accounts of visiting or planning to visit colleges. Sherrod's request was above and beyond anything we even thought possible. The reason I gave this chapter its name is because some of us settle much too soon just as we started to do in regards to Sherrod's future. We were settling into a lifestyle we believed both him and us could manage. That's the wrong approach if you are a Christ follower. God does the managing and since He knew each of us in the womb it also means he knew what he purposed for each of us to do in life. We had no idea that God was trying to do something beyond our understanding. The amazing thing about this journey is that He kept moving the stop sign each time we thought we had reached the end of the road. He used Sherrod to get it done despite the fact we were moving in the direction of settling. I will admit, although Ann and I were thankful for what God had done, we lost focus on believing God for total healing for Sherrod. We had gone through so many ups and downs and I think we really started to believe what some of the doctors had predicted. They thought we could reach a place where Sherrod's condition could be manageable. It was looking as if they were correct. We weren't having big setbacks and life was beginning to take on some sort of normalcy.

We were unaware that God was using each small victory along the way as stepping stones to something bigger. This is why it's so important not to fall into traps of believing your plight in life should be like someone else's. Remember, God fearfully and wonderfully made each and every one of us. He also gave everyone a life print that is custom made just for you. Yes, you are just that important to Him that He purposed for you to be different. Many have missed out on the cards of life that were dealt; chasing a life that wasn't theirs to live. God wanted to do more so He put the will in Sherrod to do and be more. He was also showing the school system and his parents that absolutely nothing is too hard for God. He had not dealt Sherrod the cards either we or the school was handing out.

In your search for what you believe God has for you, I would caution against falling into a belief that your plight in life should mirror someone you admire or despise. There is nothing wrong with moving in the direction of someone you admire, and it's also perfectly fine to stay away from paths you have seen or heard cause setbacks. The remarkable thing about outcomes is just what this chapter represents. What God has for you is for you and when others tell you what can't happen because of your past, don't accept it. Psalm 75:6 says that promotions come through God. He exalts you to where He wants you to be in due season. It matters not if you are being considered for a promotion on your job or to another level in your life; it comes from God, not man. Do yourself a favor; take a look at the cards of life you are currently holding. Ask yourself a very hard question. Are these the cards I'm supposed to have or do they belong to someone else? If in your heart of hearts you know you are following the leader for the wrong reason, do an about face and seek a new direction. You have a custom made life to live and although it may be similar, it was not purposed to be a carbon copy.

As we shared in this chapter, Sherrod was in a program that had not witnessed any of its students moving on to college. He was trying to pave the way for others that had the same dream. This was turning from a impossibility into a possibility.

Like with every first, Sherrod was chosen to be the first to challenge that status quo. Never settle your life based on what the surrounding voices or systems are whispering in your ears. They may be friends or loved ones who love you very much and mean you well. You have an inner voice which is the Holy Spirit that is crying out for you to take a long look at the cards of life you are holding and ask that question. Is this My Hand? God wants to do exceedingly and abundantly above all that we can ask or imagine. It's the only way you will get to live your best life.

# Chapter 9

## Pushing the Envelope

Here we were talking with teachers and counselors about Sherrod possibly entering college. Understandably, there were concerns on both sides. The high school courses he had taken were not strong enough to prepare him for college. Also, Ann and I didn't have a strong enough faith to believe college was an option, but Sherrod did. God used that act of courage in Sherrod to pave the way for other doors to open. As we started to seek other possibilities, other things started to unfold.

We are unsure exactly when, but it happened one morning as Sherrod was getting ready to walk out the door for school. As with most mornings, he was hurrying and running late. Ann and I were trying to make sure he wasn't forgetting his routine, and in so doing, she asked the question that became the result of this book.

As he grabbed his book bag moving through the house quickly, Ann asked, "Did you take your medicine Sherrod?" He nonchalantly replied, "I haven't taken that medicine in weeks, Mom." Ann and I looked at each other in amazement and fear. To be totally honest, it was mostly fear. All we could recall were other times when he had not taken the medication! Oh boy, we have a problem! This was not a child any longer; this was a growing teenager that could easily destroy a home if an episode occurred at this stage of his life.

How many times has your past experiences influenced your present dilemma? If you respond with guilty, so am I. I believe we all do it. That's why we call them experiences, right? They are supposed to help us gain a better understanding of how to address things if ever that type of situation should arise again, whether it was bad or good.

We tried to encourage Sherrod to take his pills, but he refused and told us that he was fine and didn't need any pills. When he told us he had not taken his meds for weeks, listen to me, our past experience told us, there is no way he could have missed weeks of not taking this medication without there being a setback or reaction of some sort. Therefore, we cannot always draw on past experiences; they may lead us into doubt and fear if we are recalling a bad one. Even if you experienced something good, as we discussed earlier, it does not mean God is going to show up the same way every time. Yet on the other side of this situation, it opened the door to the miracle. God took our past experiences with this disorder - and I mean ALL OF THEM - and made it totally impossible for us to ignore the fact that if what Sherrod was telling us was true, God had intervened and performed a miracle. That is God's character! He will set a situation up so strategically that when you go to investigate, all you can say is: *"it's a miracle!"* This was one of those moments. Remember we had consulted with some of the best specialists in the country, institutions such as: Walter Reed Medical Center, John's Hopkins Medicine, and Hershey Medical Center. None of them indicated that Sherrod's T.S. would go away. They were all trying to find ways for us to cope. God made sure we had come to the end of ourselves and resources so that we could not give credit to anyone else for what we were about to witness through Him alone.

For the next few days and weeks, we watched our son very closely just to see if we saw any signs of a setback. We talked with Shawn, and he indicated that he had not heard any sounds or seen any movements associated with his T.S. for what he considered awhile. We asked him to keep us informed of any changes he might see or hear.

One of the most amazing things about this entire miraculous process is that our boys were acting as though the miracle was no big deal!  I have now come to realize that they were already walking out the miracle.  It wasn't new to them, only to us.

The days would go by, and we would check off each day that there were no episodes.  No noises and no thumps from his feet which were all previous indicators of his T.S.  At some point, we decided that it was time to schedule a checkup to make sure a doctor could verify what we hoped to be true.  We made an appointment with a nearby specialist who indicated that while she could not tell us what happened, there were no signs of T.S.!  She also told Sherrod that if he experienced any symptoms relating to T.S. to just give her a call.  The doctor was at a loss for words, and we believe a bit skeptical having seen Sherrod's chart with all the information she was seeing about his case.  I can only imagine it must have been pretty difficult to believe after hearing from us that we were not experiencing anything on the chart.

I cannot explain how inexplicably happy we were at this news! Could this be true? Could the miracle we had prayed about for so long finally be here? Had Jesus walked in the room and validated our prayer request through this doctor? We so wanted to believe it! We were so tired of being tired. We were holding on to hope and trying to let go of fear. As time moved past that initial appointment, we walked on eggshells keeping our fingers and toes crossed. I should have trusted that God was doing what we asked, but I'm just being totally transparent when I say that I was working with shaky faith. I was trying to cross all of the t's and dot all of the i's in hopes that there were no setbacks. It would be embarrassing to run out prematurely proclaiming a healing. I was trying to prevent that from happening. I believe God meets us where we are, and this was just where I was. I'm not sure when we stopped counting the days before we conceded that God had indeed performed a miracle. We were so glad that the running and the biting had stopped; everything else became much easier to deal with. Those two things (running and biting) would have been game changers for sure.

I don't think we said anything to family and friends for a short period of time, but I will say that every time we heard a sound in the house that reminded us of the past, we froze in anticipation of what might be coming next.

That's common. Past experiences bring back remembrances. But it never happened! Do you hear me? IT NEVER HAPPENED! God was true to His promise, and He was not finished. Sherrod went on to participate in track and field and football during the remainder of his high school years. Not only did God do all of that, but upon completion of high school, our son was accepted into college. While nobody, from his guidance counselor to us, believed college was in his future, God did. Sherrod enrolled into a traditional college and quickly became aware that it was not a good fit for him. Undeterred, he transferred to an Art Institute, where in 2014 he received his Bachelor of Science degree in Digital Filmmaking and Video Production. He is currently making his way and progressing in an industry that is often known for being very challenging and difficult to sustain as a career. He is focused and making connections that will prayerfully put his name on the movie screens soon.

Recently, Ann and I were having a conversation with him about his career goals, as we do with the entire family once a year. Although the projects have been few and far in between, he has no plans of quitting. I recall a telephone conversation we received from him while we were riding in the car to an event. He initially called to ask what most kids do when they leave home. I know that they actually never leave home, and they also never leave your pocket. So, this was a pocket call, and I could sense, like most parents, the big question about money would come up. After approximately fifteen minutes of what I call *set up talk*, there came his question about us possibly loaning him a few dollars until he could get paid. We asked him a question about possibly trying something else so that he could start to build a solid work foundation. We asked him where and when he would decide to *draw the line* in the sand and just take on a 9-to-5 job. He indicated that there was no line, and he was determined to live out what he called his purpose. I deeply admire and respect the tenacity and drive he possesses to get what he wants, and I have no doubt that he will be a very successful film producer or whatever else he puts his hands to do. He has gained the fortitude to believe he really can do all things with Christ's help. What you have read is an account of a nine year making of a miracle. Why was it so important for me to tell it? First and foremost, it is very important that I tell this story because the Bible says let the redeemed of the Lord say so (Ps 107:2).

I'm doing what God requested that we do if we are redeemed. It was also very important to tell because I believe my family needed an account on record of the journey God took us on many years ago so that it can be shared for many years to come. It's important to tell this story because I also wanted to record how our family felt, how we moved, and how we responded to God in a very difficult time in our lives. I want family and friends to know that it's okay not to be perfect in your faith walk and still receive a miracle. It's fine to wonder if God has forgotten about you and even have questions for Him without questioning Him. I wanted my sons, Shawn and Sherrod, whom I love dearly, to know that their dad was a man full of everything they will probably experience as they continue to grow as men. I want them to know that they played and are still playing a vital role in my growth process as a man and as a follower of Christ. They were given a gift through this experience that is a part of their history and legacy. It is important that they know that God will meet them wherever they are in life because He is the giver of life. I want them to know that no matter how dark the nights may get and how desperate they may feel, there is only one place to turn when they believe there is nowhere else to go, and that is to God. I want them to understand that there is no time limit on the delivery of miracles. Wait, I say, on the Lord! I want them to carry this testimony with them on their journey through life. If there should come a time where they need reassurance that God is still with them, I want them to pick up this book and thumb through these pages. I guarantee on whatever page they should land, they can hear God speak.

There is also one last amazing and undeserving gift God gave our family. He took a marriage that was in ruins and deepened our love for one another in ways that only a crisis like T.S. could bring. He allowed Ann and I to find what was missing in our marriage. We found a deeper love that we could only find in our valley. He didn't stop there. He also created a bond in the family that can never be broken. God loved us so much that He chose a crisis that would be the instrument He would use to heal our marriage, the family, and Sherrod. It sounds crazy, right? It is! Everything God does is crazy good. Remember my prayer? *"God, if we don't get help, we are not going to make it."* Well God heard me, and He answered. Since then, Ann and I have established a faith-based, non-profit called Growing Every Mind, Inc. whose mission is to focus on the health and welfare of the family using biblical principles. We also counsel couples seeking to prepare, repair and restore their marriages. We are so grateful for what He did for us.

Ann was the glue that kept and held the entire family together throughout many of those "dusk 'til dawn" mornings. To be totally honest, she is still the glue. It's appropriate to say, from my mother who modeled for me what faith looks like, to my wife who graciously grabbed the baton and is modeling it today, both have shaped my life in too many ways to count. I'm grateful for what they have done to help chart my life. There are also a few good men that have done the same that I will mention in other projects.

Many of you reading this book may be in some pretty hopeless situations. You might believe there is no way out and you might as well give up, right? Lean in. I have something to share. God will never leave you or forsake you. He was here before you arrived, He is here through your present situation, and He will be here much after you are gone. So, this book was written for you, as well! I need to let you know that God is not a respecter of persons. In other words, I'm not God's favorite, even though I say that a lot. I say things like that because I find it incredible that a God that has so much going on would find time to take care of little old me! I'm not famous and I'm not rich.

What I do have is an inheritance handed down from my heavenly Father, and that's all I need! God being my Father places me in the position of family. If you are a family member, it comes with certain rights and privileges that others don't have. I don't have to be rich; He is (Ps 50:10) I don't have to be famous; He is (Phil 2:10). And because He is both rich and famous, all I need to do is let others know who my father is and that seals the deal every time. Listen friend, there is a reason you picked up this book! You know there is something pulling on your heart and telling you not to give up, that this is not the time to throw in the towel! I may not know your specific story, but I do know this: God does not love me or our family any more than He loves you and yours. He wants to do for you what He did for us. I'm not saying God is going to answer your prayer just like He did ours, but what I am saying is God's purpose in your current situation is not to harm you, but to give you hope and a future (Jer 29:11). God sees your situation past where you are and into a future that is full of hope. I pray you were encouraged by what you read. I pray it pushes you past your quitting point into determination. In closing, like some of the preachers say when they are about to wrap up a sermon, I tell you this: It's in the valleys of our lives where we are made strong, and it's on the mountain tops of our lives where we get to take breaks. If you are on the mountain top, take a deep breath, look around you, and relax for a little while. Prepare for the descent into your next valley. If you are in a valley, know that you are being strengthened and fortified. This too shall pass; you are coming out. There is a mountaintop on the horizon. The West Family went through some valleys, but every valley was named and chosen for our good and for His glory. I know it really gets difficult trying to stay positive waiting on God to deliver His promise to you. Wait on Him and receive it. We waited many nights and many days. As we referenced throughout this book, and in Eccl 3, there is a beginning of a thing, but there is also an ending. There are ups and there are downs, there are mountains and there are valleys.

Finally, my friend, there is dusk, but morning is coming. Look for the dawn. If you are experiencing a hard time right now and things don't seem like what you prayed for, I want to encourage you. Our journey became easier when we took the focus off what we were seeing and leaned into what God said. He promised to heal Sherrod; He didn't tell me how He would do it. The dusk of your trial awaits the dawning and deliverance of God's promise. Never give up, never give in. When you don't understand God's ways, trust His character. He did it before, he'll do it again. You are going to win!

Wink West
**#gobegreat**

## Outtake

I really wish this story was full of heavy faith nuggets for you to grab. Actually, it's more of the opposite. This is why God's grace is so amazing. The song writer Dottie Rambo wrote, *"He looked beyond all my faults and saw my needs."* It's a true love story about the extent of God's love towards a family that was hanging in the balance on so many levels. God remembered what Ann and I asked Him to do through our marriage many years ago. We had drifted into deep waters and His way of honoring our request was by sending us help in the form of a health challenge.

I recall so vividly how we responded to the news about Sherrod not taking his meds. God was pushing us away from our past experiences into what we had been asking Him for all along, which was healing. We couldn't see it coming so we were holding on to what we had become accustomed.

What is God asking you to let go of that you are holding onto so tightly? Let it go! Believe me, what you are about to let go of is only an experience moving towards a promise. You have been praying for the promise and if it arrives you may not be able to receive it unless you let go of the past experience. Drawing on our experiences was sending us into fear and not faith. Our past experiences were preventing us from knowing that God had moved on our behalf. We were praying for a miracle and didn't know that the miracle had already been granted. It reminds me of the story in the Bible the way Luke tells it in chapter 24. Luke recalls the account of the disciples grieving the death of Jesus after the crucifixion. They were so fixed on their most recent experience witnessing him being beaten and murdered so badly, that they took their eyes off of the promise of the resurrection. When the miracle (Jesus) appeared right before their eyes, they didn't realize it. It doesn't get any clearer than what you see. They didn't see it manifested because their eyes were fixed on something they witnessed in the past.

I know it's difficult, when you think about some of the past bad experiences that caused pain and trouble, not to think just maybe it may happen again. That's where we were. Actually, I believe I may have thought, "not again" when we thought we heard something familiar from the past.

In order to receive the blessing, there has to be a shift in our awareness and belief that the blessing that was promised is on the way. We blew it again! The shift had not taken place and we were not aware that the promise had been delivered. Also, once again, God did not charge our shaken faith to our account. If you read Luke 24, you will see where Jesus told the disciples to examine his hands and feet and to touch him since they were having trouble believing it was him. You may recall what Thomas said before he saw Jesus after the resurrection. He declared that he was not going to believe any of what the disciples were saying about Jesus being alive until he witnessed it himself. Ann and I were much like Thomas. We were having trouble believing Sherrod was fine without taking the meds. Remember my thoughts earlier. We have to let the past experience go if we are going to receive and experience the miracle that is on the way. The disciples had to do it, and so does everyone else.

This is our story! It was written to give someone hope and to remind others that it's never too late to share yours. I started putting pen to this project years ago. It has been redrafted and even lost after being half complete. At that time, I did not have a back up copy so I became discouraged and suffered from what they call writer's block. It lasted for a few years. I just could not muster the energy to say it again. I now realize that my writer's block was actually a God block. He wanted to write it His way and in His time. There were some missing pieces that were yet to be developed that would show even more of God's amazing grace. He paused the ending so that the full display of His healing power could shine through. Now that you have heard ours, go tell yours. The world is waiting to hear what God has to say through you.

Lastly, we thought it would be interesting and insightful to ask our sons to write about their experience. Here is what each had to say:

## Shawn and Sherrod's Outtake

I really can't recall when it all started. My mom says that she remembers me and my neighborhood friend playing outside with Sherrod. I came to her saying that Sherrod was blinking a lot and shaking his head. I don't really remember that, however my memory as of today is when my brother and I were on a trip to Busch Gardens, Williamsburg, VA with the family and seeing him blink a lot. At the time, everyone was saying that it may be allergies and we went on with the trip. When we got back, it seemed like the symptoms would become different and compounded. The blinks and the head shakes were added by grunts. The grunts would then be added by screaming fits. Tourette syndrome (T.S.) is what I was told my brother had. I had never heard of it before and would get what little information was given to me by my parents as they spoke with doctors and researched what they could.

It is amazing to think, this was during the beginning of the internet and Google wasn't the major search engine it is today. Information wasn't readily available about T.S. It seemed we were learning about it through the experience. I laugh now but, I remember that my brother is the reason our family purchased cell phones.

I can't remember if it was a weekday or weekend but everyone was home. My dad was getting ready to go to work which was thirty minutes away from our home. My brother was fine and it was a normal day. As my dad leaves for work my brother starts to have one of his episodes! I ran out to catch my dad who was down the road. I wasn't fast enough. We needed him and needed him now! I ran back inside to tell my Mom that I couldn't catch dad, he was down the road. She reluctantly said alright and tried to manage my brother as best she could.

At this point with his T.S., because of the medication he was on, he would have hallucinations and biting spells. I had gone upstairs to my room because my Mom said that she could manage. About ten minutes later I hear her softly call for me. As I walked down the hall, I see my brother has my mom in a headlock and biting her hair. I could only think this was a scene out of the Exorcist! She calmly said, "call your dad at work, he should be there by now, and tell him he needs to come home." I picked up the phone and spoke with my dad. Needless to say, he made a 30-minute trip home in twenty. Sidebar, he still drives like that. He gets my brother off of my mom and pins him to the ground. I see Sherrod growling, hissing, and trying to bite my dad. He prayed and prayed over Sherrod as he tried to get out of my dad's grasp. By the grace of God, he calms my brother down and gets him into the car. Car rides mixed with the music would normally calm my brother enough to get him to sleep.

Looking back on my brother's sickness and what my parents had to handle, I don't believe I really understood the magnitude of what they were dealing with. I felt like I was on the outside as a spectator most of the time. I witnessed Sherrod having screaming fits that would last all night to my dad having to take him out for a drive to calm him down and get him to relax.

I remember a hospital visit to a Medical Center to leave my brother there overnight for observation. I saw how concerned mom and dad were for my brother and not giving up hope of him getting better. Doctors said time after time that they were not sure of what his full prognosis was and prescribed another medication they believed would work. Our family was told that this would be Sherrod's life and we would have to manage it as best we could. The prayers came from churches everywhere, even Pastor Donnie McClurkin himself. It is crazy to see their faith through it all.  I felt helpless and that I couldn't help in any way.

My mom and dad came together to manage what they could with my brother.  I felt during this time my job was to pretty much stay out of the way.  I had great friends in high school and they lived close by.  I was also in different activities and sports to keep me busy.  I felt guilty at times because I had opportunities to get away from the madness that was happening at home.  I thought that if I kept busy away from the house it would help mom and dad by not having to worry about me.

It is incredible to say that we are on the other side of it now and to know how Sherrod is completely healed from it all.  It is a true testimony to how God can perform a miracle in your life.  I thank God that Sherrod is completely healed, also for cell phones.

In all seriousness, I do believe that this was a journey that could have broken a person, but my brother stood in there and kept fighting.

I thank God for my parents; I don't think they could have gone through that without each other. It would have been easy to give up when you don't see the light at the end of the tunnel. I guess if you know where your light comes from while you are in the tunnel you know to follow that light. This light was God who knew that if we walked it out, He would bring us from darkness to light. Guess what, that light helped us persevere and push through. Everyone didn't know we were in a tunnel, but everyone knows now we are walking in the light.

Sherrod declined to write about his experience and decided instead of putting his thoughts to pen, he would wait and make the movie. I can't wait to hear and see his story.

# The Evolution of a Miracle

The Years of Discovery

H.S.Basketball Team

College School of the Arts

On the Job in the Film Industry

# <u>Where to find Wink</u>

**Facebook**

**Growing Every Mind, Inc**. (G.E.M., Inc.)

https://www.facebook.com/growing.e.mind

**Gmail:** Growingem@gmail.com

**Instagram:** GROWING.E.MIND

Made in the USA
Columbia, SC
16 February 2025

53936987R00109